Country Houses

Country Houses

A.B. THORNE

ILLUSTRATIONS BY RICHARD TOGLIA

A ROUNDTABLE PRESS BOOK

 HOME PLANNERS, INC.

A Roundtable Press Book

Directors: Marsha Melnick, Susan E. Meyer

Assistant Editor: Marguerite Ross

Illustrations and Interior Design: Richard Toglia

Book and Cover Design: Michaelis/Carpelis
Design Associates, Inc.

Photography: Jessie Walker

Designs for Interior Photographs: frontispiece,
Marilyn P. Akins, room design; page 17,
Sheldon Hill, architect; page 18, Sue Suster,
carpet design; page 26, Janice Russell, room
design; page 29, Deborah Shein, room design;
page 30, Darlene Lowe, room design

Published by Home Planners, Inc.
23761 Research Drive
Farmington Hills, MI 48024

Charles W. Talcott, Chairman
Rickard Bailey, President and Publisher
Paul S. Kitzke, Editorial Director

First printing, August 1988

ISBN: 0-918894-65-4

COUNTRY HOME STYLES

The history of the American home is rooted in the belief that we, as Americans, can live in houses that express our free will and individuality. Although most American houses basically conform to specific elements of shape and form in plan and in attention to detail, personal preferences and tastes prevail. In this book, country houses have been distilled to three styles: the Cape Cod cottage; the American farmhouse; and the center-hall classic Colonial. These designs have endured because they capture our imagination, connect us to our architectural heritage, and prove eminently practical to live in. To sum up each style: the Cape Cod cottage is warm and cozy; the farmhouse is nostalgic and friendly; and the center-hall classic is serene and dignified. All three add up to: "Welcome!"

TABLE OF ONTENTS

GUIDE TO COUNTRY HOME STYLES

COUNTRY HOME DECORATING IDEAS

HOME PLANS

The Cape Cod cottage was born as a snug defense against wind and cold, salt spray and stinging sand. The spit of land elbowing into the Atlantic Ocean south of Boston that gave this beloved American home design its name endures ferocious storms; houses built here had to withstand a harsh climate. The colonists who settled on Cape Cod in the late 1600s and early 1700s made their living by fishing, and so spent their days at sea. Applying the skills they had acquired as ships' carpenters to the construction of their homes, they crafted their houses to be as neat, taut, and weather-tight as their handsome wooden boats.

The Cape Cod cottage—a compact and unadorned box capped with a gable roof—usually faced four-square into the prevailing wind, crouching low on massive hand-hewn oak sills which served to stabilize the structure on the sandy soil. The Cape's chunky post-and-beam armature was overclad with rugged, rough-sawn shingles; narrow planks trimmed and sealed the four corners of the house. A plank door and two small windows were the only distinctive features of the facade. The planes of the house and roof were unbroken; the lack of a roof overhang allowed the wind to slam against the house and sweep up and over it without inflicting any damage.

The earliest Cape Cod-style house, like all primitive dwellings, was an elemental shelter. It comprised a single room that embraced all domestic activities—eating, sleeping, and socializing. Architectural historians classify this Cape, which predates 1700, as a "half-house" or "honeymoon" house, as it was really too small to accommodate a family. Because its shape was so simple, though, the house could be added onto easily.

By 1720 the style had evolved into a "full" Cape. With the introduction of the chimney, the plan altered somewhat as the rooms focused around it. The chimney and its hearths became the center of the house. It braced the structure more securely against winds and warmed the house, both directly by the fire and also by radiating warmth from the masonry mass to adjacent rooms. A chimney often boasted as many as three fireplaces—one facing each of the two main rooms flanking it, and the third opening to the keeping room which ran the entire width of the house behind the main rooms. In many schemes, a tiny room—the "borning" room, reserved for childbirth and illness—was tucked in alongside the keeping room. By the mid-eighteenth century, the Cape expanded to a second story. The strength and bulk of the chimney enabled flooring to be laid in the attic, affording separate sleeping quarters away from the constant hubbub of family life.

Two other design features increased

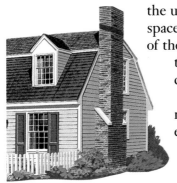

the upstairs living space: the alteration of the roofline and the addition of dormers.

The gambrel roof, with its extra, hipped pitch on either side of the roof ridge, expanded the actual space under the roof and eliminated the claustrophobic feeling fostered by steeply canted eaves. The dormers (from the French word *dormir* for sleep, or *dormoir* for dormitory) were upright windows installed to protrude beyond

the roofline, adding space and light to the upstairs room.

Windows were enlarged in later versions of the Cape—as they were, of course, in all houses. As glazing techniques became more sophisticated and windowpanes commercially available, home builders could install more and bigger windows. The multipaned

double-hung sash remained the norm for the Cape, but shutters, which had first been placed on the inside of the house to shield it from wind, were moved to the exterior of the house and turned into window accents. The chimney moved from the center of the house to whatever position suited the owners, especially when stoves and, later, furnaces supplanted the fireplace as a source of heat.

The Cape Cod, although it was never displaced as a house design, erupted in popularity during the 1920s and again in the 1950s. The Cape was—and is—the American dream "starter" house. As suburbs spread and new families blossomed, the Cape flourished, always retaining its feeling of coziness and warmth. The American affection for the picturesque and charming has assured that the Cape Cod cottage remains a true American favorite.

The American farmhouse—practical yet picturesque, noble yet nostalgic—embodies the soul of our agrarian heritage and frontier. In terms of design, it evolved into two distinct strains, both equally popular throughout the generations.

One type, in fact, derives equally from the Cape and the Colonial. It is a symmetrical house, well proportioned and well balanced, but not so imposing as its Colonial antecedents. The second farmhouse type developed after the mid-nineteenth century and is a more casual cottage-type house, asymmetrical and with a more ornamental appearance.

Both versions share one very distinctive and one very American feature: the front porch.

This porch, in its most basic form, consisted of a simple portico approached by a short flight of steps, or perhaps just a step or two. The portico had been added on to protect the front door, but gradually grew more ornamental and imposing. The more elaborate entry was a symbolic gesture of welcome to visitors. The sheltered entrance said, "Come in. This house will harbor you, will keep you safe."

Once the portico was established as a practical but beautiful addition to the house, it seemed only natural to expand it. Once it was seen that the porch could be a hospitable outdoor room, not simply a transition from street and yard to house, it assumed a special identity of its own.

The architecture of the porch and portico derived from Greek motifs. Thomas Jefferson and others who had traveled to Europe brought back sketches of these motifs and applied them to their own homes. The portico recalled Greek pilasters and pediments; the porch, extending the full width of the facade of the house, was a graceful, informal evocation of the classic temple colonnade.

As the porch began to dominate the face of the American farmhouse, the front door literally fell into shadow; it no longer required a grand architectural statement. As a result, the cross-buck with lights, a charming door with rustic appeal, generally relegated to the back of the house, was moved to the front instead.

Basic Colonial-style farmhouses developed regional variations during the eighteenth and nineteenth centuries, especially in the mid-Atlantic region and in the South. The Southern plantation house

took on a character all its own in response to the climate of the region.

The plantation-style farmhouse was one room deep to facilitate cross-ventilation. The front door aligned with the back, and the hall between the two was wide. During the summer months both doors would be kept open to allow breezes to circulate throughout the house. Larger windows increased the flow of air; many first-floor windows, in fact, ran all the way to the floor so that they could open onto the porch or veranda.

Porches were constructed both at the front and along the rear of the house—and sometimes all the way around. In the South, the porch, or veranda—in some regions called a piazza or galerie—was a necessary outdoor room because the heat was so intense throughout the summer. Porches also guaranteed shade to the interior. Some plantation houses added upstairs porches, which were used for sleeping and for domestic work such as sewing.

Plantation houses erected near rivers were often raised on stilts to elevate them in case of flooding. Raising the house also ensured air flow beneath the house, cooling the interior from below.

Northern farmhouses, developed primarily along Colonial lines, added porches and dormers to the beloved garrison-, gambrel-, and gable-roofed designs. In the Plains states, the gable end of the house was turned to the street and a wing added to form an L. The porch was tucked into the elbow of the L, running the length of the wing itself. In this way, the porch sheltered only a single room, or at most two rooms, as well as the entry. A secondary porch might have been added to the side or the rear of the house to shelter the kitchen door, or the porch might actually have wrapped the front and side of the entire wing.

The Plains farmhouse matured as manufactured components became more readily available throughout the country. Lumber was in seemingly endless supply, and planks, boards, and all millwork could be easily transported by the new railroads.

Balloon framing, based on multiple studs, made construction easy, and materials could be combined attractively. In the latter half of the nineteenth century, board-and-batten siding—a vertical planking—became as popular as time-honored clapboards back East. Wood was mixed with stone and brick or stucco and sometimes with timbers in contrasting tones.

Following pattern books much like this book of home plans, builders began to individualize their farmhouses by playing with particular features—not just the porch. The dovecote, for example, became a standard fixture, as did the cupola and weathervane. In contemporary versions, wrought-iron hinges on the garage door remind homeowners of attached barns and other outbuildings of the farmsteads of their ancestors. The American farmhouse endures because it combines the charm of the past with the necessities of today.

As settlers became more accustomed to the environment and climate of the New World, and as they became more affluent, they wanted to express their new status, their sense of security and prosperity, with larger and grander homes. By the early eighteenth century their houses no longer hunkered down against the elements; houses in the original thirteen colonies were no longer merely shelters for survival.

The basic center-hall Colonial evolved quite simply and logically from one boxlike room with an attached chimney to two rooms flanking the chimney, with a little hall or vestibule at the entrance. The two rooms could both be heated from a single source and the expanded house presented a pleasant and symmetrical facade to visitors. This so-called I-plan expanded upward and outward with later additions. It easily doubled and quadrupled—from two rooms over two to four rooms over four. In later versions the center chimney was transposed to an end wall and a second chimney added onto the opposite end wall. By such logical multiplication, the center hall expanded substantially, gaining stature with the addition of a grander staircase.

As the colonies grew more prosperous in the decades leading up to the American Revolution, British influence on domestic architecture became more and more apparent. British carpenters and cabinetmakers emigrated to our shores while wealthy Americans traveled to Britain and the Continent, bringing back ideas about architecture, interior design, furnishings, and way of life. They also brought back pattern books—the equivalent, in those days, of a home plan book.

This was an era when rules governed behavior as much as they did design. Rational thought extended from manners to dress, and fashions in dress paralleled fashion in architecture. What better way to express status than in one's home?

This was the beginning of the era of the four Georges in England; the architectural style of the period was called, naturally enough, Georgian. This style employed classical ideas of order as translated through the doctrines and buildings of the Italian genius Andrea Palladio and British emulators such as Inigo

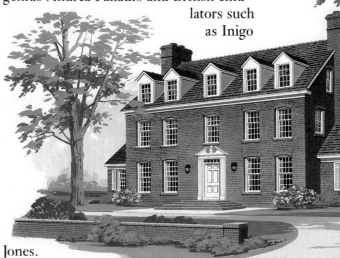

Jones. The style was disciplined and balanced—genteel, composed, and assured. The Georgian house was massive and solid, an apt symbol of new-found prosperity in America. The symmetrical facade centered on an imposing, often ornate entrance. The front door, frequently paneled, was set into an ornamental surround that recalled ele-

ments of Greek temple design, and the entrance was often braced by pilasters and crowned with a pediment. Elaborate pediments might be broken, with or without a scroll. A transom or fanlight brought light into the house while further defining the entry.

The Georgian facade, like that of any center-hall classic, was punctuated by graceful double-hung multipaned sash windows accentuated by shutters. The windows aligned, row to row, and in later versions the windows in the top row were set into dormers. The roofline of the center-hall classic varied. The roof could be

a simple pitched gable, a gambrel, or even a hipped style. The dormers protruded from the roofline in stately procession.

There were now typically two chimneys, both wider and taller, removed from the core of the house and transferred to the end walls. Sometimes they would be doubled, with twin sets of paired chimneys replacing the standard single pair.

Balance and order prevailed inside the house as well as out; the facade mirrored an equivalent concern for harmony in the interior plan. The Georgian center-hall classic allocated specific functions to specific rooms. The formal rooms swept off to the right and left of the center hall at the front of the house; the informal rooms were relegated to the rear. In the houses of the newly affluent, the hall no longer served as reception room and dining hall, but instead alerted the visitor to the status of the homeowner. The hall and stairs, in addition, effectively separated the public and private zones of the house. Visitors could be ushered immediately into the parlor, the room reserved for formal entertaining. The word "parlor," in fact, derives from the French *parler*, which means "to talk"— polite conversation.

The strictest interpretations of the Georgian style were found in the mid-Atlantic and Southern regions, where estates and plantations were far grander than land holdings in New England.

Brick and stucco, the materials of choice in the South, translated more effectively to grand-scale architecture than the wood indigenous to New England homes. After the American Revolution, the Georgian style evolved into the less imposing Federal style. Federal houses ("Federal" refers to an independent, all-American design) retained balance and symmetry, but were stripped of extraneous ornament, presenting a pleasing, unpretentious facade. Inside, the plan expanded to include rooms to accommodate various modern conveniences, such as closets and indoor "privies."

The center-hall classic, in its less stately form, responded readily to ethnic and regional adaptations. For example, the Dutch Colonial, a sturdy dwelling built of rugged stone and concentrated along New York State's Hudson River, had a unique flared roofline that was compatible with the center-hall form. Throughout New England, the center-hall classic, typically crafted all of wood, appeared as a more intimate house than its Southern counterparts. The facade was sheathed in clapboards or shingle instead of brick or stucco. The chimneys did not protrude from the end walls, but were contained within the wall-line to conserve heat.

After the Industrial Revolution, building materials could be factory-produced in quantity and shipped anywhere. Once the railroad connected cities and towns, people became more mobile than ever before. During building booms at the end of the nineteenth century and again during the 1920s and 1950s, people looked to their architectural heritage to inspire but not copy new homes.

Country homes lend themselves to a variety of decorating treatments. Here and in the pages that follow are variations on a country theme, ideas that suggest the great versatility of country design.

Of all features in the entrance hall, none says welcome more eloquently than a beautifully detailed staircase. In a spare hall (*photo opposite*), a subdued, subtle Williamsburg green paint emphasizes the gracious lines of the staircase, and especially the carved ends of the risers. The same green rides up the wall-hung banister and chair rail. The front door, by contrast, is unpainted and highly polished, like the floors. Antique Oriental runners add a special refinement to the room. A dropleaf secretary, too, is an elegant accent and can function as a work space. Wall sconces light the space, supplemented by candles when the mood strikes.

An all-American hall (*top right*) plays on slightly toned-down colors of the flag—red, white, and blue. The floor paint is a lustrous marine type that can take the abuse of wet boots or shoes. The blue continues on up the stairs and banister. The red draws attention to the front door and the walls. A trailing-vine paper pulls all colors together.

A cozy stair hall with a flower-dappled wing chair (*bottom right*) encourages lounging. The wood paneling is untouched except for occasional buffing. Walls and risers bear a coat of sunny yellow. Stenciling, repeating the curves of the riser carvings, leads the eye up the stairs. A bold rug covers most of the floor, adding to the feeling of warmth. A tall case clock is conveniently situated for all comers and goers. The grapevine wreath on the door is a permanent reminder of outdoors.

. . . .

All activities begin in the house at the entry hall and its staircase, which together connect rooms and levels—as well as public and private zones.

14

The large kitchen can be daunting, both in creating an efficient work space and in decorating it so that it feels cozy. Rule One: Break up the overall space into self-sufficient zones, linking them visually to lend harmony to the room as a whole. The intimacy of both the work and dining areas of this country kitchen (*photo opposite*) belies its grand scale. Each bay window re-inforces the feeling of warmth and light. Terra-cotta relief tiles act as clay transoms for extra visual warmth and cue visitors to the casual Spanish decorating motif. Over the com-mercial range (which dominates all three versions of the kitchen) hangs a custom-molded hood on brackets, again ac-cented with tile. Wall ovens next to the range increase the oven count to four, and the marble-topped counter is perfect for large-scale baking. Two phones face each other, one in the menu center and another close to the window seat in the dining area. Comfort at the dining table is assured, as every chair has arms and thick, plumped cushions. Recessed lights zero in on all areas of the room, yet do not distract from the spacious feeling.

A delicate, restful spirit infuses the French provincial ver-sion of the kitchen (*top right*). Pale tone envelops the space; walls, floors, and base cabinets comple-ment each other per-fectly. Against this serene backdrop, a huge copper hood hangs over the range. In the eating area, fresh blue-checked linen covers the win-dow seat, and the blues are picked up in an embroidered linen tablecloth and scrub-painted rush-seated chairs.

The intense colora-tions of an Amish quilt, translated to a painted floorcloth, dictate the palette of

. . . .

The eat-in kitchen, whether large or small, defines most clearly the "home-within-a-home." So much takes place here—eating, chatting, cooking, relaxing, —it is little wonder that the kitchen is called the heart of the house.

the third kitchen (*bot-tom*). Each wall is sin-gled out with color. The commercial range is capped by a massive black metal hood whose steel fences corral a collec-tion of platters. Black on the base of the peninsula causes the counter to appear to float. Each translu-cent green pendant lamp targets a spe-cific zone in the room; the green teams with similarly colored stools at the counter. Cherished banister-back chairs, softened with canvas cushions, pull up to the dining table.

One of the coziest rooms in any house is the library or den. An English country-style library (*photo opposite*) bases its decorative scheme on the many moods of the color claret. Claret paint washes the paneled walls and is dramatized by neat white trim and mantel. The classic Chesterfield loveseat, tufted and studded with brass nailheads, is upholstered in rich glossy leather, just like those found in men's clubs. Paisley, another print used often in British homes, covers the window valance and panels and a fat ottoman, which slides neatly under the overscaled coffee table. Wooden Venetian blinds drop down from behind the valance; the wood matches the floor.

. . . .

Because it is geared for hospitality, the den— or library, or game room— becomes the magnet and the focal point for cheer and conviviality. Casual comfort is always the goal in decorating this cozy room.

Patterns, big and small, play against each other and against white paneling in a comfortable den (*top left*). A carved oak mantel surrounds the brick fireplace, above which hangs a treasured framed landscape. A Hawaiian quilt drapes over the loveseat; the bold pinwheel pattern teams up with the equally graphic hand-painted coffee table. A blue gridded rug runs underneath the table, and draperies of a similar hue hang by rings from a pole that reaches across the entire window wall.

A casual, sunny game room (*bottom left*) boasts panels painted in sunny yellow. A bank of bookcases built under the windowsills holds books, albums, and favorite family games. Unmatched antique chairs gather around an expansive candlestand-style table used primarily for games. Roll-up shades at the windows become almost invisible when pulled up all the way. A rattan easy chair, outfitted with canvas pillows displaying an oak-leaf design, offers a refuge for reading.

Tucked under the eaves, a bedroom is naturally cozy and inviting. Guests especially appreciate such an ambience. The porcelain tones and delicacy of paper and fabric, one reversing the other, set the mood in a charming carpeted haven (*photo opposite*). The print was inspired by a museum document. A chipper blue-and-white check acts as a compatible coordinate. The pencil-post bed had its finials lopped off to fit under the sloping eaves—and looks more casual as a result. Swing-arm brass lamps hang at the perfect height for reading. To filter light from the broad window, a shade pulls down behind the shirred valance. The pig pillow, a favorite barnyard beast, is a comfortable country collectible and handy backrest as well.

The vibrant graphics of a star motif add drama to the attic hideaway (*top right*). Ceiling stars hover on a deep-blue skyscape over the pretty, cottage-style bed with carved head and footboards. The bed is plumped with a down comforter in soft, blue shades. The hooked rug displays four-pointed stars inside a grid of sober-hued lozenges. Stars appear again on the chest made of inlaid wood; this star is derived from a familiar patchwork pattern. Simple casement curtains add privacy.

In an earth-toned aerie (*bottom right*), the bed is pulled up close to the window and set on the opposite wall. Made of faux-bamboo, it is capped with a canopy of the same fabric as the draperies and dust ruffle. The quilt harmonizes with the muted plaid used to upholster the armchairs nearby. Another rendition of wood: the white birch base to the round table. Candles add a romantic note at teatime or at bedtime.

A sanctuary removed from bustling family areas, the attic bedroom offers respite and quiet for its occupants, whether they are the parents of the household, a teenage child, or invited guests.

A spacious bathroom is a joy! Like a dark shawl, a dense floral wall covering wraps a Victorian-style bath (*photo opposite*) above wide beaded-board wainscoting. Over-scaled fixtures—tub and pedestal sink—appear as generous here as they must have in the hotel they once inhabited. A parquet floor soothes wet feet; several coats of sealant have made the wood impervious to drips and moisture. The brass-and-glass shelves and racks accent the room; the shelf holds a cache of antique perfume bottles and sterling silver grooming accessories, as well as a gilded table clock. Globe lamps glow in the room from wall and ceiling. A narrow tiered shelf is topped with beautiful hydrangeas.

Mirrors on two walls visually double the

. . . .

Given ample space, the bath assumes the status of a well-loved room; this is very desirable, because the bath, above all, serves to enhance feelings of well-being.

size of a nostalgic bath (*top left*). Wide boards laid on the horizontal form a wainscot; deep hunter green paint above the wood is matched by like-colored towels and bath rug. The claw-foot tub and pedestal sink, bowl, and pitcher are all enameled reminders of the past. Polyurethane protects the stenciling on the floor. A dresser, cut at the top like a dry sink, stores extra towels, washcloths, and soaps. The corner lamp reflects in the mirrors to create more light.

Peach paint and mahogany-toned wood create a flattering ambience for a bath (*bottom left*). The wood, used for continuous base cabinets under the sink, is recreated in the bath surround. Floorboards mirror boards used in the panel inserts. A broad floral border girdles the room at chair-rail height, running behind the towel rack that hangs from the wall cabinet. The sink and countertop were formed of a single piece of synthetic marble. Thick, newly crafted hooked rugs rest in front of both tub and sink.

For a narrow corridor kitchen to feel unconfined, it must be opened up visually. In a floral-bedecked kitchen (*photo opposite*), a pattern of grids amplifies and adds energy to the space. A trellis across the ceiling meets the botanical grid on walls and soffits. The floral pattern, repeated in drapery and upholstery fabric, is soft in tone, a suitable backdrop for collections of porcelains. The floor is easy-care, resilient vinyl tile—a look-alike, as is the "butcher-block" laminated countertop. The pretty draped table, accented with miniature watercolors, is a lovely spot to linger over coffee or late-night snacks.

A pristine, low-key kitchen (*top right*) takes its cue from its bold and clean checkerboard ceramic tile floor. The blue and white pattern sparkles underfoot, its drama accentuated by a long rug of contrasting shades. Pale walls create a visual counterpoint to all-wood cabinetry. Wrought-iron pulls, like the chandeliers, are authentic early American touches, as is the cast-iron kettle. The canted range hood has a lip that doubles as a shelf for favorite antique plates. A hanging shelf also holds storage for compatible collectibles.

The great outdoors inspired a green and white kitchen (*bottom right*). Abstract pine trees march along the top of deep green wainscoting, enclosing the eating area in a forest. The green continues to the base cabinetry, while the overhead cabinets match the white wall above the wainscot. Resilient flooring simulating fieldstone is a practical alternative to the real thing. Sleek black-glass-fronted appliances are visually linked by the black toeplate running under the base cabinets; black is also featured in the star-centered bull's-eye floorcloth under the gateleg table near the window. A sheer curtain, drawn to one side, is a romantic change from a traditional heavy curtain. Restaurant accents in the kitchen include the copper range hood, copper cookware, and handsome, classic bentwood chairs.

With two walls facing off against each other, the corridor kitchen compresses the work elements—appliances, cabinets, and countertops—into a tightly organized, efficient work area where every inch matters. If space permits, an eating area, especially with a window, adds personality and warmth to the room.

The well-engineered master suite includes a sitting area and plenty of storage. In a garden-fresh suite (*photo opposite*), a ribbon trellis establishes the background for the main room, while bright yellow paint sets off the sitting alcove. Twin closets with a window seat between them were built around the main window in the room. Delicate floral designs accent closet doors and are repeated on the quilted bedcover. A wicker rocker sits on a floral-patterned dhurrie rug, whose mate accompanies the camel-back loveseat in the lounge area. A straw hat and French provincial armchair bring spring indoors all year round.

A sleigh bed turns parallel to the wall in a master suite that

. . . .

The perfect suite consists of bedroom, bathroom, spacious closets, sitting area, and room for exercise, hobbies, and work, a place where the heads of the house truly feel they can get away from it all.

incorporates a full-scale eating area near the window seat (*top left*). A border defines the ceiling line. Mirrors set into the walls in the window seat bring in lots of light and amplify outdoor views. A rag rug, pieced and seamed to fit, reaches almost wall to wall. A fringed swag in the window adds a graceful touch to the comfortable room.

In a bed-sitting room with a more European flavor (*bottom left*), closet doors and window-seat platform simulate panels crafted in Germany and Austria. Like many of the cupboard beds in the Old Country, the window seat adds curtains for privacy. Similar draperies pull across the window in the sitting alcove, unifying the two areas. Twin wall sconces provide supplementary illumination in the window-seat nook; other sconces accent the walls in both the main room and sitting room. As a final flourish, a soft pastel flat-weave rug effectively pulls all colors into focus, anchoring the spacious master suite.

With double French doors, a den or family room can be thought of as a converted sun-room; if doors are left open during summer months, the room lives up to that reputation! Extra-high ceilings and white walls expand the feeling of light in a cheerful retreat (*photo opposite*). The room steps up to the rest of the house and, through the doors, leads to a patio and garden. Simple lustrous floors, left uncovered, add to the airy atmosphere, as do the casual twig armchairs and table. Twig is a bit scratchy, so puffy pillows provide comfort. These coordinate with the upholstery chosen for the deep plush loveseat. A hoosier chest standing in for storage and desk proves that any beloved antique can find a cheerful place in a home and heart.

An alternative to the den, a music room (*top right*) functions perfectly in this location a bit away from the hubbub of family life, especially during hours set aside for practicing the piano.

Twin wicker loveseats and a comfortable Windsor offer friends and visitors a chance to enjoy the performance or to sing along with the piano player. The sun comes into this room perpetually, as the walls are painted pale yellow and the upholstery picks up on a brighter yellow in its zesty zig-zag print. Trees grow and flourish in such an environment, as do flowers. Parquet tiles, polyurethaned to repel moisture, echo the geometric patterns of the fabric and the panels on the face of the upright piano. Carriage-light sconces are apt reminders of the outdoors.

Clear, crisp geometrics and deep cool colors refresh a spare, yet intimate haven (*bottom right*). The focal point, a bold,

. . . .

The family room is probably the most public space in the house after the kitchen, so it's particularly nice when it is so casual that no one feels intimidated about putting up his or her feet and simply hanging out—just for the fun of it.

graphic quilt hung above the sofa, lures the eye to the seating group. Patch pillows and a kilim runner carry through the geometric theme. A diminutive wing chair and fan-back Windsor can be moved around at whim, depending

upon the gathering. Pictures, hung low, emphasize a cozy scale; the wide frieze at the ceiling also draws the ceiling down. Another trick, painting the ceiling and frieze in bright tones, reinforces the room's pleasantly warm feelings.

The mood of a corner bedroom is distinctly happy when it harnesses sunlight from two sides. The flower-dappled wall covering in a shuttered bedroom (*photo opposite*) seems to be as nourished by the sun as the room's inhabitants. The louvered shutters were painted the same temperate green as the mini-print fabric used for the dust ruffle and pillows on the bed. At the foot of the bed, a folded antique four-block quilt appears to have

been lovingly washed many times, its colors bleached to soft hues. Underneath, a scalloped Marseilles-type spread pulls up to the pillows. A primitive linen press and a blanket chest, still in its original paint, provide extra storage in the room, as does the bentwood hat rack standing near the dresser. The bare floor, glowing with a matte sheen, is freshened by a pair of rag rugs. Because rag rugs tend to slip, these are anchored by thin rubber pads. A twig rocker and ladderback armchair offer seating options.

Hyacinth-rich lavender cloaks the walls of a romantic corner bedroom (*top left*). A much paler lavender adds romance to the bed skirt and window swags. To temper sun at the windows, the swags mate with

. . . .

The complement of upstairs rooms usually includes a corner bedroom, which is a wonderful space because it can capitalize both on the light and cross-breezes, and on the lovely architecture of its windows.

thick wooden Venetian blinds, which match the Victorian dresser. A bedcover appliquéd in vines and fruit is draped atop the polished brass bedstead; a coverlet lies at the foot of the bed. The floor, painted green, is partially cloaked with a jewel-toned needlepoint rug and banded in black and lavender. Twin armchairs with a French feel are at opposite sides of the room, but are light enough to carry to a table for breakfast or midnight cocoa.

In a child's room (*bottom left*), bright crayon colors key the entire scheme. Slick red outlines the windows to contrast with the white walls and wood floor. The windows have cafe curtains, which a youngster can easily open and close. On the floor lies a new hooked rug featuring a barnyard scene. An antique corner cupboard, missing its top doors, stashes toys; clutter hides underneath! A small-scale rocker is perfect for soothing dolls to sleep. The ceiling fan and light unit provide light as well as breezes.

Plan B2596, page 44

THE CAPE COD

Snug and cozy, yet versatile in plan, America's "first house" adapts to any site.

First floor:

919 square feet

Second floor:

539 square feet

Cozy yet comfortable, this Cape provides space for all the needs of a couple or a small family. In fact, the house could be enlarged to accommodate a wing as more children join the first-born; the side hall is a natural link to any future extension. The heart of the house is a country kitchen, centered by an island large enough for two to dine at. Both the kitchen and the adjoining dining room open to a large back terrace. Upstairs, each of the two bedrooms has its own bath, and a linen closet is situated next to the center stairs. Just inside the side entrance to the house is a powder room and an extra closet that could be converted to a laundry. An extra surprise under the roof: a bonus storage zone tucked in next to both bedrooms at the front of the house; these would be enjoyable hiding spots for children's play, too.

The living room opens into the dining room, permitting a view of the terrace through double glass doors.

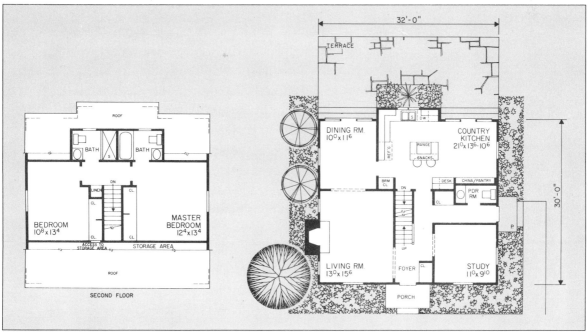

SECOND FLOOR

ROOF

BATH | BATH

LINEN | DN | CL

CL | CL

BEDROOM
10⁸ x 13⁴

MASTER
BEDROOM
12⁴ x 13⁴

CL

ACCESS TO
STORAGE AREA | STORAGE AREA

ROOF

32'-0"

TERRACE

DINING RM.
10⁰ x 11⁶

S | DW

REF'G | RANGE

SNACKS

COUNTRY
KITCHEN
21⁰ x 13⁶-10⁶

BRM
CL

DN

DESK | CHINA/PANTRY

CL | PDR
RM

30'-0"

LIVING RM.
13⁰ x 15⁶

UP

FOYER | CL

STUDY
11⁰ x 9¹⁰

P

PORCH

First floor:

976 square feet

First floor expanded:

1,230 square feet

Second floor:

744 square feet

This basic half-house Cape has been planned for expansion so that a young couple can think ahead to adding on for a growing family. The planned addition provides for two new wings to accommodate a future study with adjoining covered porch and for a garage; these additions add 254 square feet to the house. Later, the attic over the study could be converted to a fourth bedroom, and still later, the terrace could be covered over and closed in to create a family room. The side door in the basic plan would lead conveniently from the kitchen to the garage. A powder room off the foyer is a gracious touch in so compact a house. The linen closet upstairs, which backs up to the two baths, could be neatly converted to a mini-laundry with the addition of a stacking washer and dryer. Despite its diminutive size, the house features full-scale authentic architectural details on the exterior, such as 9-over-9 sash windows and a massive center chimney.

A brick fireplace, with matching brick floor, runs along the interior wall of this ample country kitchen.

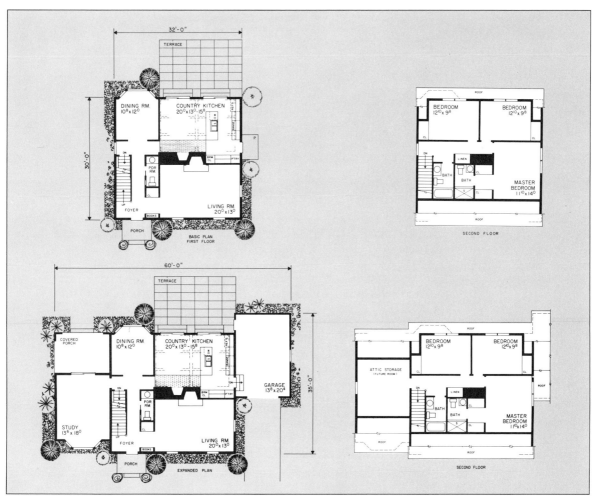

First floor:
1,137 square feet

Second floor:
795 square feet

The design of this Cape Cod, although extremely snug and compact like its eighteenth-century antecedents, thoughtfully provides plenty of light, even to the center of the house. The kitchen extends as one large room, over the snack bar, into an expansive family room. This area is warmed by a generous fireplace. Both the family room and the living room open directly to the center hall, which also leads into the dining room at the back of the house. The huge bay window illuminates formal daytime meal celebrations in the dining room and also draws light into the hall. Upstairs, two bedrooms share a windowed corner bath. The master bedroom boasts both a dressing room leading to its own bath and a big walk-in closet. A study downstairs could be converted into yet another bedroom; a full bath is adjacent. A hall, also adjacent, effectively closes off this private zone from the busier rooms downstairs—a welcome feature when relatives or friends come to visit.

On the first floor, the entry leads directly to the dining room, the living room, and the family room.

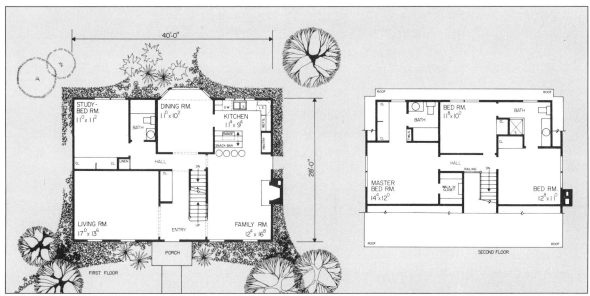

First floor:
1,020 square feet
Second floor:
777 square feet

The facade of this three-quarter version of the Cape belies its amply proportioned interior. At the rear of the house, a wide gable elevates the second story to accommodate full-scale windows, thus affording plenty of extra space—and headroom—to the upstairs baths and third bedroom. Two front bedrooms have windows to the sides as well. A special feature of this plan is its spacious, eat-in country kitchen, with beamed ceiling, window seat, and raised hearth. In the formal living room a second fireplace—placed back to back to the one in the kitchen—abuts a built-in cupboard reserved for display of treasured books and collectibles. Exterior details include a five-paned transom over the entrance and a pair of carriage lamps.

A corner fireplace in the large country kitchen faces a spacious bay window.

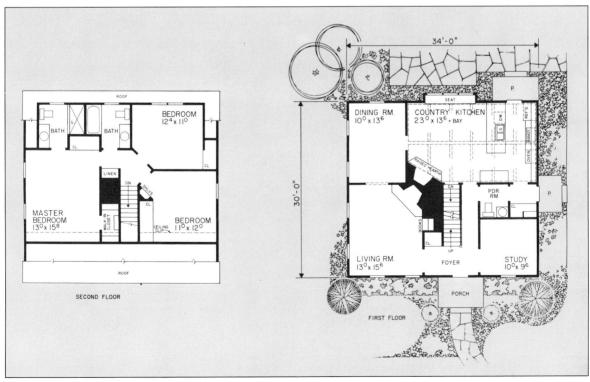

SECOND FLOOR

BEDROOM
12⁰ x 11⁰

BATH   BATH

MASTER
BEDROOM
13⁰ x 15⁸

BEDROOM
11⁰ x 12⁰

FIRST FLOOR

DINING RM.
10⁰ x 13⁶

COUNTRY KITCHEN
23⁰ x 13⁶ + BAY

34'-0"

30'-0"

RAISED HEARTH

PDR.
RM.

LIVING RM.
13⁰ x 15⁶

FOYER

STUDY
10⁰ x 9⁶

PORCH

First floor:
2,012 square feet
Second floor:
589 square feet

In this "telescoping" Cape, each section of the house looks as if it had been added on, yet all form a coherent, harmonious whole. The bonus here is a separate upstairs master suite that accommodates a study-lounge as well as a dressing room and bath. Truly a hideaway, this suite is virtually invisible from the street, allowing the mother or father of the family to feel really "away from it all." Extra storage is also located upstairs. Downstairs, three bedrooms share a luxurious bath. At the other end of the house, a full laundry and washroom are convenient to the kitchen and garage. In fact, this area can also function as a mudroom for a family. A covered porch leads from the garage into the laundry as protection against inclement weather.

The living room, connected to the dining room, is located off the entry.

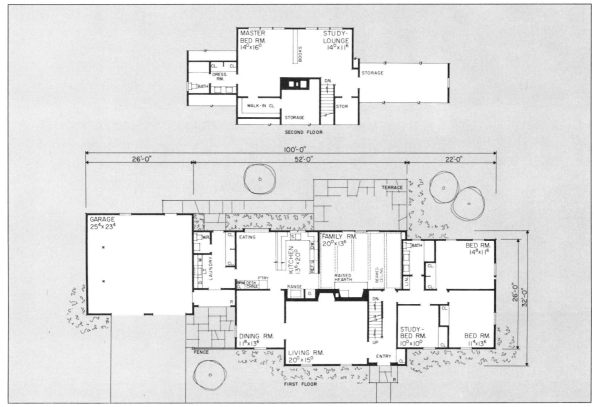

MASTER BED RM. 14⁰x16⁰

STUDY-LOUNGE 14⁰x11⁶

BOOKS

CL. CL.

DRESS. RM.

BATH

DN.

STORAGE

WALK-IN CL

STORAGE

STOR

SECOND FLOOR

100'-0"

26'-0"

52'-0"

22'-0"

TERRACE

GARAGE 25⁴x23⁴

W.R.

CL.

EATING

S.

D.W.

FAMILY RM. 20⁰x13⁶

BATH

BED RM. 14⁸x11⁶

CL.

D.

W.

LAUNDRY

CL.

KITCHEN 13⁶x20⁰

REFG.

RAISED HEARTH

BEAMED CEILING

LIN.

26'-0"

P'TRY

DN.

32'-0"

CL.

DESK

RANGE

D.

CL.

CHINA

UP

P.

DINING RM. 11⁸x13⁶

STUDY-BED RM. 10⁰x10⁰

CL.

BED RM. 11⁴x13⁶

FENCE

LIVING RM. 20⁰x15⁰

ENTRY

CL.

P.

FIRST FLOOR

First floor:
1,489 square feet
Second floor:
982 square feet

In this tidy Cape, the entire rear portion of the house is devoted to a large family gathering area that in Colonial times was called the "keeping room." Here the family comes together to cook, dine, or simply relax by the fire. The entry hall is particularly spacious in this plan; a powder room separates the entry from the formal dining room. A laundry off the kitchen boasts a long counter for sorting and folding dry clothes. Upstairs, the master suite includes a huge walk-in closet as well as a dressing room with twin vanities. The bath shared by the other two bedrooms has a linen closet alongside.

One large area contains a family room, an eating area, and the kitchen, in the tradition of the "keeping room."

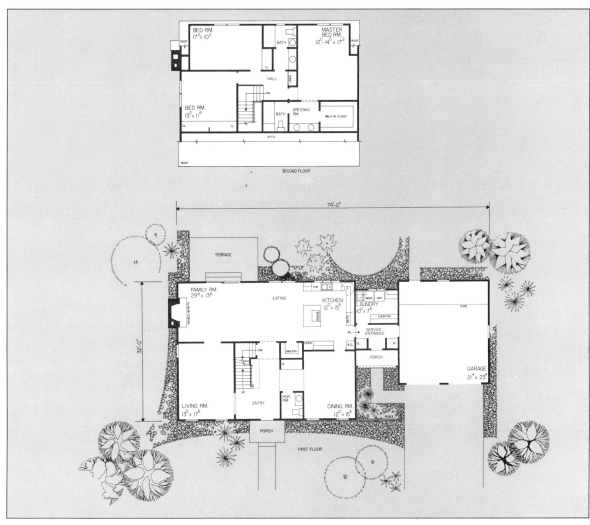

SECOND FLOOR

FIRST FLOOR

First floor:
1,157 square feet
Second floor:
875 square feet

A flawless example of a center-hall Cape, this plan is hard to match because not an inch is wasted. The generous living room leads directly to a dining room, which has a bay window to harness as much light as possible. The study assures complete privacy when totally shut off and makes use of two closets to buffer noise and commotion from foyer and living room. The family room, with its raised hearth, is a sure focus for many activities and is convenient to the kitchen and laundry room. Upstairs, two bedrooms and a walk-in closet are illuminated by dormer windows. The two upstairs baths, like the third bedroom, have full windows facing the backyard. The entrance to the house is inset slightly as a protection against rain and snow.

The family room, with beamed ceiling and raised-hearth fireplace, is connected to the kitchen.

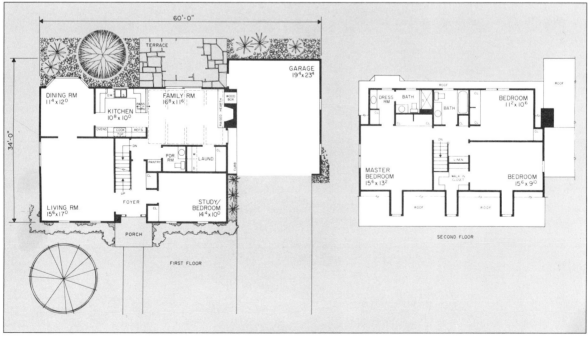

FIRST FLOOR

SECOND FLOOR

First floor:
1,632 square feet
Second floor:
980 square feet

The deep roof overhang on this tidy Cape attractively exaggerates the pitch of the roofline while protecting both family and visitors from inclement weather. The entry is indented slightly further as an additional air-lock, but is transom-lit to pull light under the overhang into the entrance hall. The kitchen, with its breakfast nook, faces the front of the house while the family room and laundry alongside open to the rear. With this layout, the children can run indoors and out without bothering their parents while they are cooking, visiting over coffee with friends, or working at the nook-based desk. The fireplace in the living room is flanked by windows facing the side yard. The downstairs bath may be used both as a powder room and as a guest bath, since the study can convert to guest quarters. Upstairs, all the closets (except the linen closet) are of the walk-in type, and one has its own dormer. One walk-in closet links the house to its attic storage zone.

The entrance hall leads directly into the living room, offering a view of the handsome fireplace.

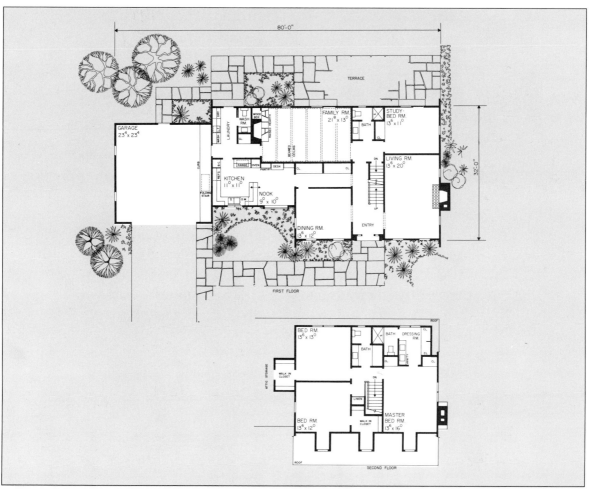

FIRST FLOOR

SECOND FLOOR

First floor:
1,136 square feet

Second floor:
936 square feet

The off-center entrance to this Cape recalls the earliest versions of this time-honored design. Long shutters and a transom highlight the doorway and a carriage light adds a graceful accent. Built-in storage greatly enhances the liveability of the house: Two china cabinets flank the door between the front hall and the breakfast nook in the kitchen, and twin closets do the same to a window seat in the family room. Such details are enticing to a family that enjoys collecting or antiquing together, for they can display all their best-loved treasures; in fact, the closets can be opened up as vitrines to highlight books or trophies. Upstairs, two bedrooms have walk-in closets, and the study, which can be used for guests, has two closets. Daylight pours into both bathrooms upstairs; one has a dormer. A cupola and weathervane positioned atop the garage roof add just the right touch of country.

The study-bed-room, located upstairs, contains two closets on either side of the window.

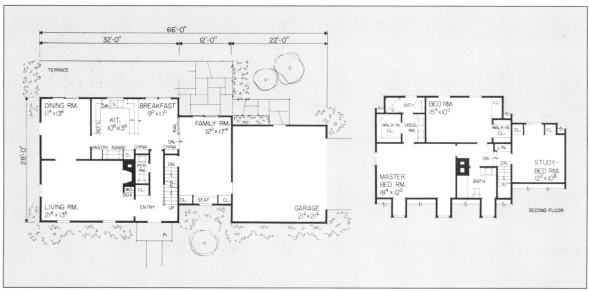

TERRACE

DINING RM. 11⁴x13⁶

KIT. 10⁸x13⁶

BREAKFAST 9⁰x11⁰

FAMILY RM. 12⁰x17⁴

PANTRY RANGE CHINA CHINA

PDR. RM.

WD. BOX CL.

LIVING RM. 21⁴x13⁶

ENTRY UP

SEAT CL.

GARAGE 21⁴x21⁴

66'-0"
32'-0" 12'-0" 22'-0"
28'-0"

BATH

BED RM. 15⁴x10⁰

WALK-IN CL. DRESS. RM.

WALK-IN CL.

MASTER BED RM. 18⁴x12⁰

BATH

STUDY-BED RM. 12⁰x10⁸

SECOND FLOOR

First floor:
1,182 square feet
Second floor:
708 square feet

This half-house—half the length of a standard Cape—
actually turns into an L to supplement the living space
with a covered porch and ample garage. This configuration particularly suits a corner lot and snugly encloses a
terrace besides. A snack bar with pass-through window to serve
the terrace has been designed just outside the kitchen. The
kitchen pantry stands next to this window and is most convenient for storing beverages and foods to be taken outdoors. The
Cape has four bedrooms, two upstairs and two down, so any
member of the family can attain maximum privacy. The family
room, which also serves as the dining area, employs a huge bay
window to flood the area with light from the flower court. If a
separate, formal dining room is desired, the back bedroom
downstairs is perfectly located for an easy conversion. There are
two fireplaces, one in the family room and another, set at an
angle, in the living room. The living room, in addition, has two
bookcases bracketing the garden window.

The fireplace in
the living room is
set in the corner.

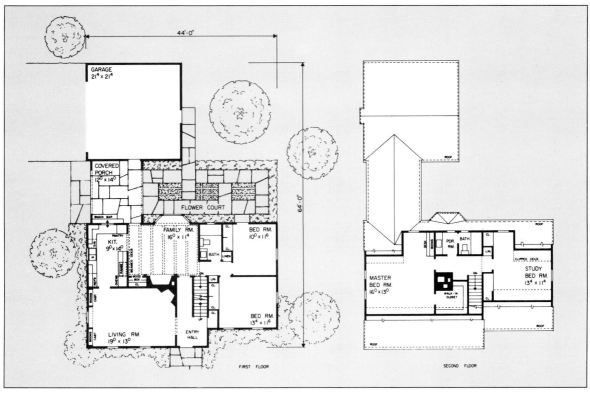

FIRST FLOOR

SECOND FLOOR

53

First floor:
1,664 square feet

Second floor:
1,116 square feet

The central axis in this one-and-a-half story rambling Cape is a gracious entry hall backing up to a massive chimney. The two act together to anchor the house and serve as a strong focal point. The garden window in the front library is flanked by two paneled bookcases, and a closet adds to the storage space in this room. A buffer zone between the library and the more active areas in the house is achieved by introducing a wide back hall, laundry, and washroom. The hall leads to the beamed family room. The living room also has a beamed ceiling, and both rooms are warmed by fireplaces. Triple dormers pull light into the upstairs. A double linen closet is convenient to all bedrooms. Charming architectural details, such as a dovecote cantilevered over a faux door into the garage, add visual excitement to the exterior, while a covered breezeway adds a practical element—deliveries can be made from the service court with no thought to weather, rain or shine.

A country kitchen, outfitted with a barbecue range, lies at the end of the generous entry hall.

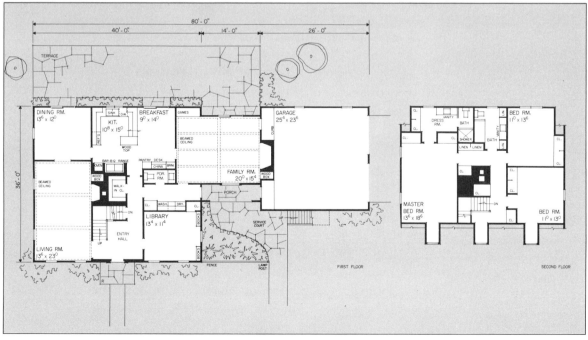

80' - 0"

40' - 0"   14' - 0"   26' - 0"

36' - 0"

TERRACE

DINING RM.
13⁶ x 12⁰

KIT.
10⁸ x 15⁰

SINK   D.W.
REF'G
WOOD
TOP

BREAKFAST
9⁰ x 14⁰

GAMES

BEAMED
CEILING

GARAGE
25⁴ x 23⁶

OVEN
BAR-B-Q RANGE
WOOD
BOX

PANTRY DESK
CHINA BRM.
PDR.
RM.

BEAMED
CEILING

WALK-
IN CL.

FAMILY RM.
20⁰ x 15⁴

WOOD
BOX

DN.

CL. WASH. DRY.
CL.

PORCH

LIVING RM.
13⁶ x 23⁰

UP

LIBRARY
13⁴ x 11⁴

ENTRY
HALL

DN.

BOOKS

SERVICE
COURT

UP

BOOKS

FENCE

LAMP
POST

FIRST FLOOR

DRESS
RM.
VANITY
BATH

BED RM.
11⁰ x 13⁶

CL.
CL.
SHOWER
VANITY
BATH
CL.

LINEN LINEN
CL.

CL.

MASTER
BED RM.
13⁶ x 18⁶

CL.
DN.

BED RM.
11⁰ x 13⁰

SECOND FLOOR

First floor:
1,182 square feet
Second floor:
708 square feet

A Cape half-house adapts handily to the demands of a growing family. With bedrooms both upstairs and down, spaces can convert, upon demand, as children grow and move away. The downstairs bedrooms, for example, can be turned into a study and guest room, or both bedrooms can combine to form a family room. In turn, the family room can be converted to a dining room. The possibilities are endless! The garage is separated from the main house by a covered porch or breezeway; in an alternate plan, ideal for a corner lot, the garage is set at right angles to the house. In this case, the sink is moved from the back wall in the kitchen to the side wall, and the back door is relocated. Special exterior details on the garage include a weathervane set atop a dovecote, and wrought-iron barn hinges that accentuate the vertical planking of the garage door.

The master bedroom, with adjoining study, occupies the entire second floor of the Cape half-house.

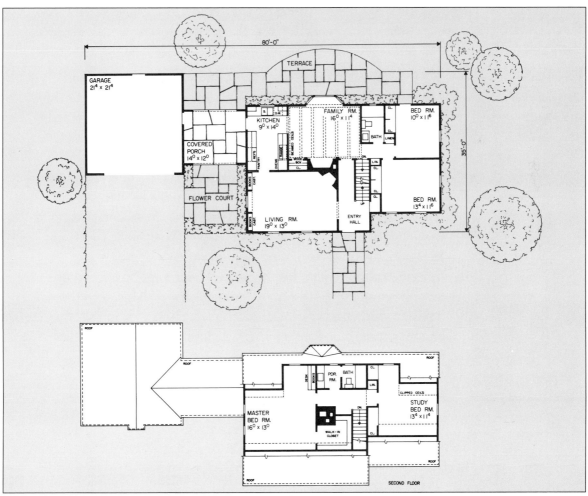

First floor:
1,344 square feet
Second floor:
948 square feet

*T*he garage wing of this Cape closely resembles the main dwelling; narrow clapboards, shutters, and lintels over the multipaned windows all match exactly. A narrow, shaded porch leads into the family room, which has twin bookcases framing the raised hearth as well as a rustic beamed ceiling. The study downstairs easily converts to a guest bedroom and is conveniently served by a bath that boasts its own shower. This bath opens to the back hall so that it can be reached easily from the back rooms in the house. Two of the upstairs bedrooms have both dressing rooms and walk-in closets. These two upstairs bedrooms can, like the master bedroom, be opened up into one commodious room by removing the wall between them. The entry downstairs provides closets on either side of the chimney wall, plus another separate closet and bookcase flanking the front door.

In the beamed-
ceiling family room,
two built-in book-
cases flank the fire-
place.

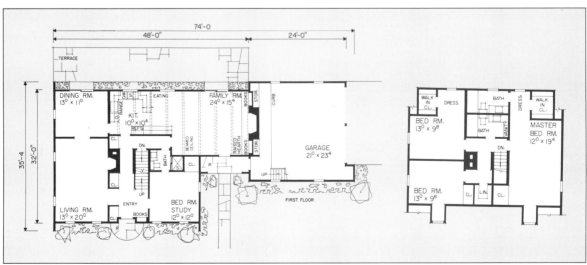

First floor:
1,388 square feet
Second floor:
809 square feet

As a variation on the Cape theme, the exterior of this charming house culls its materials from a variety of natural sources: wood, stone, and brick. The stones are particularly effective, as they set off the handsome entrance with its pairs of sidelight windows and carriage lights. The sloping ceiling in the entrance hall follows the pitched roofline, and the upstairs landing overlooks this space like a balcony. In the kitchen, a corner has been set aside as an office for menu planning and a telephone. For a parent who is at once a homemaker and an active member of the community, the office is a "command center"; for the working parent, this corner is a private coordinating post where activities are juggled on a daily basis. On the other side of this "office" wall is the laundry, with closets in between to act as a buffer against the noise of the washer and dryer. The entrance hall boasts two closets. The bedroom upstairs has a very useful walk-in closet. The linen closet, also upstairs, is situated alongside the bath shared by the two other bedrooms.

The breakfast nook, an extension of the kitchen area, opens onto the terrace by way of double glass doors.

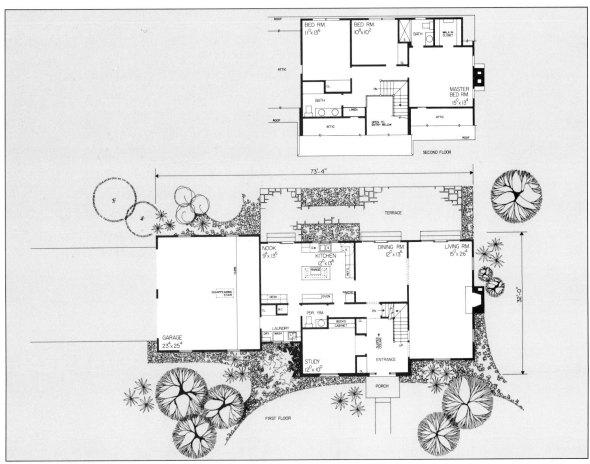

First floor:
2,683 square feet
Second floor:
1,167 square feet

In this grand version of a Cape, the entire second floor is devoted to fun! There's a playroom that can be used as a dormitory for older children who bring friends home to stay, a study, and—most luxurious of all—a sauna. This floor also has nine closets as well as a gigantic storage room. Downstairs, the configuration of rooms is both appealing and practical. Centered by a large cooking island, the kitchen is convenient to both a formal dining room and a more casual family room. There is a spacious laundry next to the kitchen, providing enough room for a big freezer plus two extra closets that can be used as pantries or for linen storage. The master suite, boasting a vanity in the dressing room and another in the bath, opens to a secluded and protected porch.

The dining room contains a spacious bow window, which is flanked by china closets.

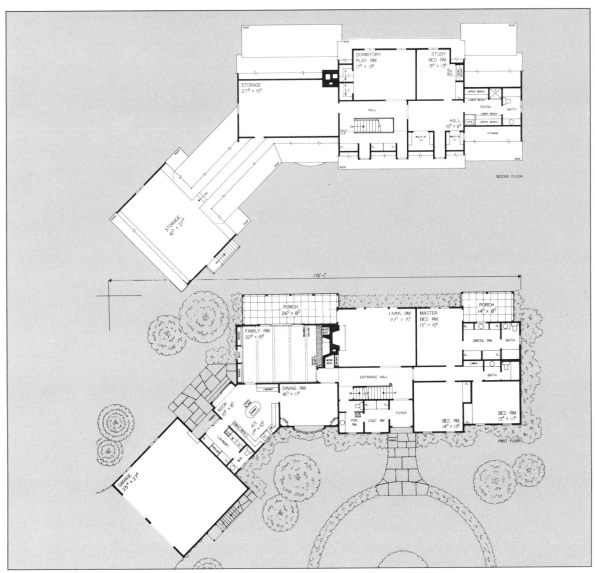

First floor:
1,211 square feet
Second floor:
747 square feet

A saltbox-style rear addition distinguishes this three-quarter Cape and provides space for a kitchen and up-to-date garage. This plan also offers a bed-and-bath suite off the foyer as well as two bedrooms and two baths upstairs. The placement of the downstairs suite ensures privacy for guests, but parents may want to reserve this area for themselves and offer the second story to their offspring. The fireplace was designed with flanking cabinetry; in the dining room the cabinets can hold a prized collection of family heirlooms and china and, in the living room, books and other personal treasures or television and stereo. Sliding glass doors lead from both the dining room and kitchen to the terrace. Extra storage space has been tucked in under the eaves at the front and back of the house. Authentic exterior details include flat keystone lintels above the windows. The plan also suggests a mix of shingles and clapboards as sheathing material.

The sloped ceiling beneath the roof-line of the master bedroom creates the cozy feeling of an attic bedroom.

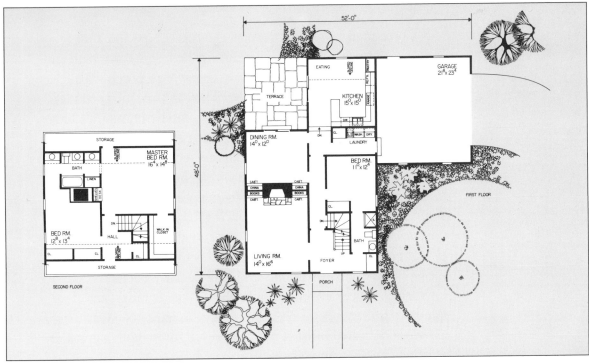

SECOND FLOOR

FIRST FLOOR

First floor:
1,481 square feet
Second floor:
861 square feet

Three wings augment the space in this snug Cape. One wing incorporates two downstairs bedrooms plus bath and a master suite above. The others enclose a porch with laundry behind and a garage. The core structure, emulating an early half-Cape, is anchored by a massive chimney. One of its two fireplaces faces the formal living room and the other warms the expansive family room. Dead-ending the living room allows a family the option of entertaining formally without interrupting other, less elegant activities, such as a teenager's slumber party off in the bedroom wing! A second bedroom upstairs has, like the master bedroom, an alcove with a built-in closet. Each bedroom has a private full bath. A half-bath serves the two downstairs bedrooms and may be used as a guest bath for parties. The back terrace links the garage, laundry, and family room, and the kitchen overlooks this area, too. All exterior doors are outfitted with carriage lights—both a gracious accent and a welcome safety feature.

A spacious beamed family room overlooks the terrace and garden beyond.

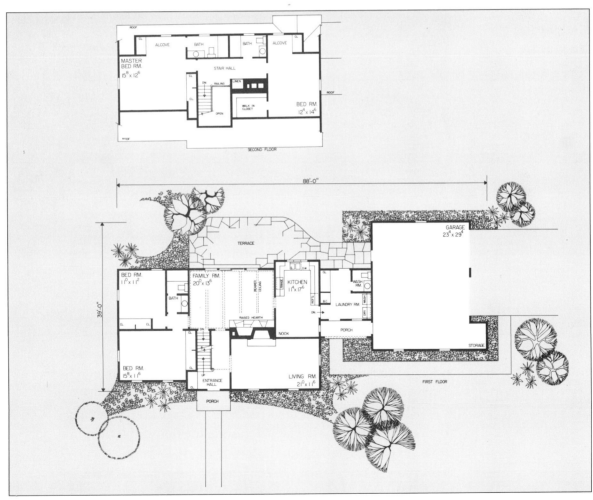

SECOND FLOOR

ALCOVE
BATH
BATH
ALCOVE

MASTER BED RM.
15⁸ x 12⁶

STAIR HALL

LINEN

BED RM.
12⁴ x 14⁶

WALK IN CLOSET

OPEN

88'-0"

GARAGE
23⁴ x 29⁴

TERRACE

BED RM.
11⁰ x 11⁸

FAMILY RM.
20⁰ x 13⁶

KITCHEN
11⁴ x 17⁶

WASH RM.

BATH

BEAMED CEILING

LAUNDRY RM.

39'-0"

RAISED HEARTH

NOOK

PORCH

STORAGE

BED RM.
15⁸ x 11⁶

ENTRANCE HALL

LIVING RM.
21⁰ x 11⁶

FIRST FLOOR

PORCH

First floor:
1,616 square feet
Second floor:
993 square feet

In order to augment living space, early Capes spawned multiple additions. This new Cape expands into two additions, one a beamed family room and beyond it, the garage. Stairs lead from the garage to a spacious storage attic. In the house, the configuration of rooms is traditional: two rooms deep on either side of a central hall. Upstairs, though, the room behind the master bedroom is a dressing area-closet. Three dormer windows upstairs flood light into two bedrooms as well as the upstairs hall. The kitchen is designed in a convenient U-shaped plan, with one leg of the U functioning as a pass-through to an adjoining breakfast nook. Fireplaces grace both the living room and family room. The hall bisects the house and then turns to conduct traffic into the family room, so families with teenagers can divert their offspring to this informal gathering place away from the more private areas of their home.

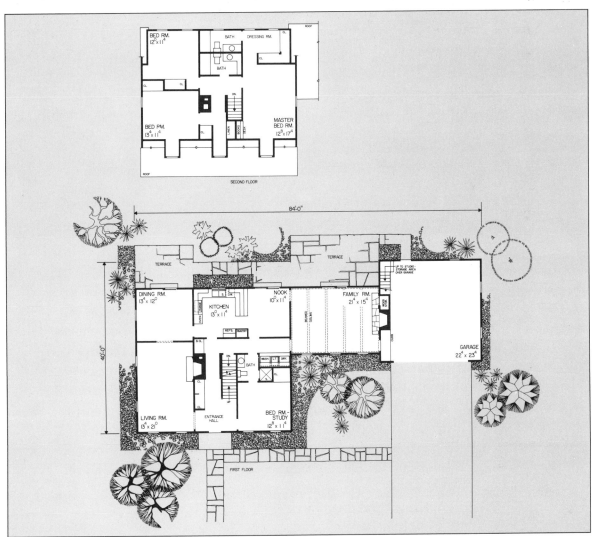

The fireplace dominates the interior wall of the living room.

SECOND FLOOR

BED RM.
12⁰x11⁴

BATH

DRESSING RM.

ROOF

CL

CL

DN.

CL

LINEN

BOOKS

BED RM.
13⁴x11⁴

MASTER
BED RM.
12⁸x17⁴

ROOF

84'-0"

TERRACE

TERRACE

UP TO STUDIO-
STORAGE AREA
OVER GARAGE

40'-0"

DINING RM.
13⁴x12⁰

NOOK
10⁰x11⁴

FAMILY RM.
21⁴x15⁴

S

D.W.

CL.

OVEN

RANGE

KITCHEN
13⁴x11⁴

REFS.

PANTRY

B. CL.

BEAMED

CEIL'G

GLASS

WOOD

BOX

GARAGE
22⁰x23⁴

DN.

BATH

WASH

DRY.

LIVING RM.
13⁴x21⁰

ENTRANCE
HALL

UP

CL.

BED RM.-
STUDY
12⁸x11⁴

FIRST FLOOR

69

First floor:
1,102 square feet
Second floor:
764 square feet

*T*he entrance to this cozy Cape, surrounded by little transom lights, welcomes one and all. Inside, the spacious entrance hall separates the formal and informal areas of the house; the living and dining rooms are to the right of the entrance and the family room and kitchen are at the back. Because the garage extends to the front, the design of the house thoughtfully provides a large laundry behind the garage that can also function as a mudroom. Thus children, pets, and groceries can be diverted to the informal zones of the house without disturbing the more formal areas. The three bedrooms and two baths upstairs take advantage of light and views to the sides and back of the house, where terraces and lawn add to outdoor enjoyment and liveability.

The spacious entry provides an open stairway that can be decorated with lighting fixtures and folk art.

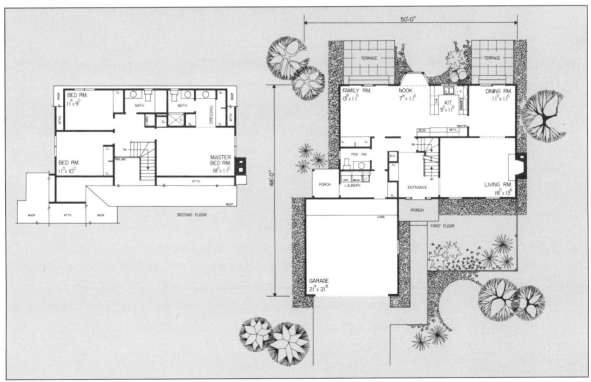

First floor:
1,500 square feet
Second floor:
690 square feet

This trim Cape is based on a telescoping design. Here the study, master bedroom, and dining wing gradually step down in depth and height from the center section of the house. Thus the second story is confined to a smaller area and the rest of the upper level is devoted to attic space. A farm kitchen, with raised hearth and beamed ceiling, is the charming focus of family activities, a place where children can do homework or craft projects while their parents supervise and prepare meals. A generous, adjoining walk-in pantry supplements storage space for the kitchen. There are two full bedrooms with a sitting room between them on the second floor; the master suite is on the ground floor. The study can be effectively shut off from the foyer so that it becomes part of the master suite and the two closets in the study can be supplemented by a third between them or by deep open shelves.

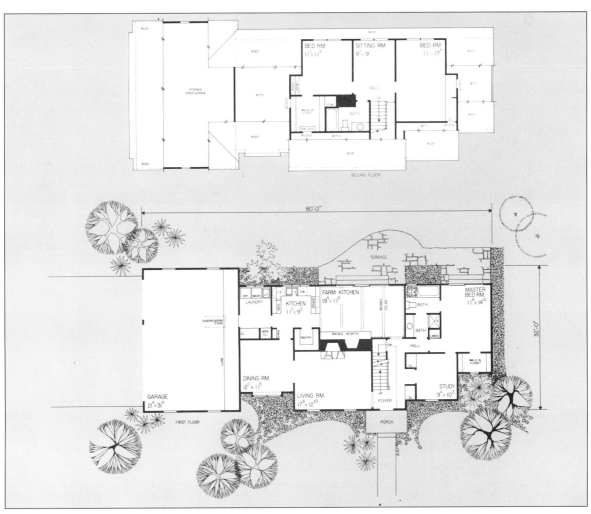

A spacious farm kitchen, with beamed ceiling and a raised-hearth fireplace, serves as a family room.

First floor:
1,217 square feet
Second floor:
868 square feet

The highlights of this compact Cape include window seats with storage underneath built into the gables in two of the upstairs bedrooms. These cozy nooks, perfect as quiet retreats from the bustle of family life, look out to the front yard. Downstairs, the massive chimney opens to two fireplaces, one in the living room and the other in the country kitchen. The fireplace in the kitchen is set at an angle in the corner of the room, and opposite is a large bay window that lights the breakfast nook. Off the living room, a covered porch offers shade during warm months. On the exterior, the chimney has a corbelled profile similar to those of Colonial days. Adding a picket fence to set off the front yard would be a charming touch.

A spacious country kitchen contains a raised-hearth fireplace in an interior corner.

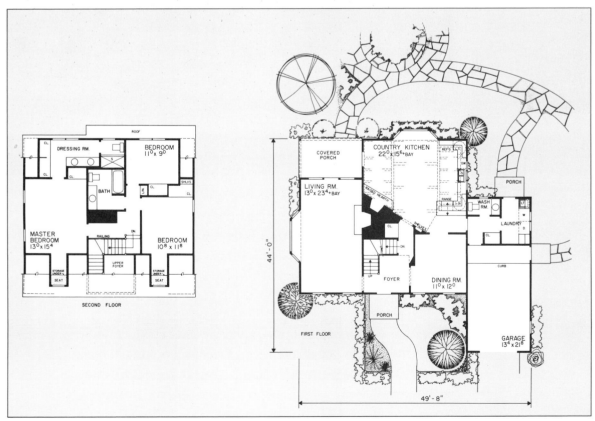

First floor:
2,563 square feet
Second floor:
552 square feet

A grandly amplified Cape takes its stylistic cue from its eighteenth-century forebears, but is expanded to include a strikingly contemporary solarium and a two-car garage. The master bedroom has two walk-in closets and a huge bath suite. For relaxation and enjoyment, the master suite opens both to the solarium and to an outdoor terrace. This house has been designed for a family that loves to entertain. It features a lovely formal dining room, but also has a vast family room with adjoining wet bar. The family room is connected directly to the kitchen by a pass-through that further increases the ease of entertaining both for the host and hostess and for their family and friends. In such a dwelling, a service hall is a must, not a luxury, and this one provides ample extra closet space as well as an extra washroom. Children's rooms and shared bath are located upstairs, out of the mainstream.

The solarium is a unique feature in this spacious Cape, a sunny area attached to the living and dining rooms and master suite.

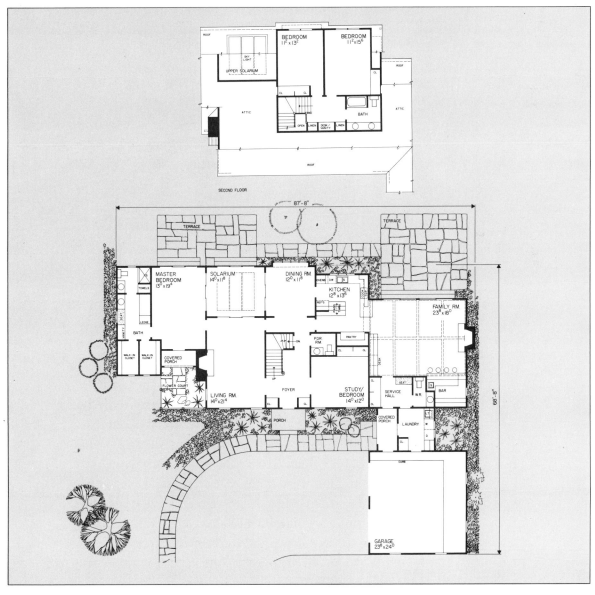

First floor:
1,218 square feet
Second floor:
764 square feet

This one-and-a-half-story Cape, with added garage for today's mobile young families, is a compact yet efficient solution to living-space problems. A traditionally styled chimney anchors the first floor, with the living room taking advantage of its fireplace and separate woodbox. On the opposite side of the chimney, in the kitchen, the range and wall ovens are set into a brick enclosure. Twin china cupboards separate the living and dining rooms; these cabinets could house stereo equipment or even a bar. Both the dining room and a breakfast room off the kitchen lead to a terrace behind the house. The kitchen between these two rooms serves each with equal convenience. For a family that enjoys entertaining overnight guests, the dining room could be converted to a den and the study could happily accommodate a sleep sofa. The garage boasts a special storage alcove and leads into the house via an ample laundry room. In the master suite, a cozy window seat offers sanctuary in the dressing area for reading or needlework.

A pair of china cabinets flank the entry connecting the living room to the dining room.

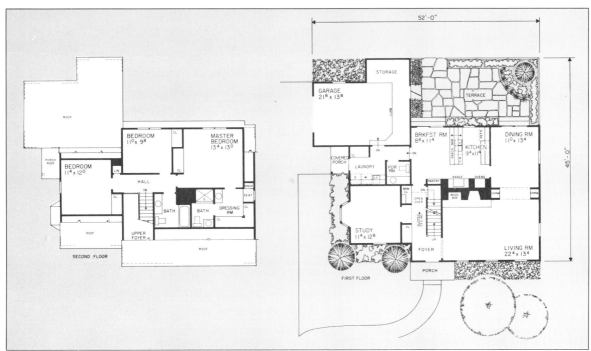

First floor:
1,634 square feet
Second floor:
1,011 square feet

In this traditionally detailed Cape, the flagstones used to pave the walkway up to the house continue on into the entry as a handsome and practical flooring surface—a thoughtful touch for an active, outdoorsy family that wants to feel as comfortable anywhere indoors as they do outside. This entry offers easy access to both the formal living room and the dining room and then leads back to a separate study and bath and on to the beamed family room. The hall turns just beyond the dining room, past a bank of closets, to reach the breakfast nook with its built-in menu planning center and the kitchen. A laundry lies between the kitchen and the family room, and opens onto the back terrace as well. This is convenient as a repository for muddy outdoor gear and gardening tools; the positioning of the laundry here assures no tracking of dirt into the formal areas of the house. Two upstairs bedrooms have walk-in closets and share a strategically placed linen closet. The master bedroom features a nicely designed dressing area with twin-sink vanity and plenty of closet space.

The living room is flooded with the sunlight from four windows.

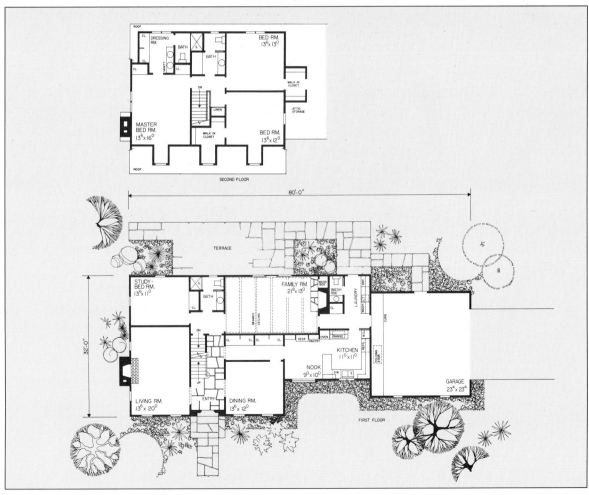

SECOND FLOOR

FIRST FLOOR

First floor:
1,830 square feet
Second floor:
1,056 square feet

The exterior of this gambrel-roofed Cape exhibits a typical variation of this beloved house style: The gambrel roof lifts the ceiling in the upper bedrooms while softening the pitch of the roofline. The soft-hued brick works in counterpoint to the vertical boards sheathing the charming garage addition. The garage conveniently gives access to a service hall and thence to the kitchen—perfect for easy transport of groceries from the car. A full laundry off the service hall is an added benefit to this design. In the beamed family room, a raised hearth is accented by a woodbox alongside the fireplace cavity. Two terraces, one behind the family room and one behind the study-bedroom, can be extended to become one long terrace if desired. All baths in this Cape are fully equipped, and storage is ample so that everyone in the family is assured plenty of space to hoard favorite belongings as well as all the day-to-day necessities.

The beamed family room contains a large raised-hearth fireplace.

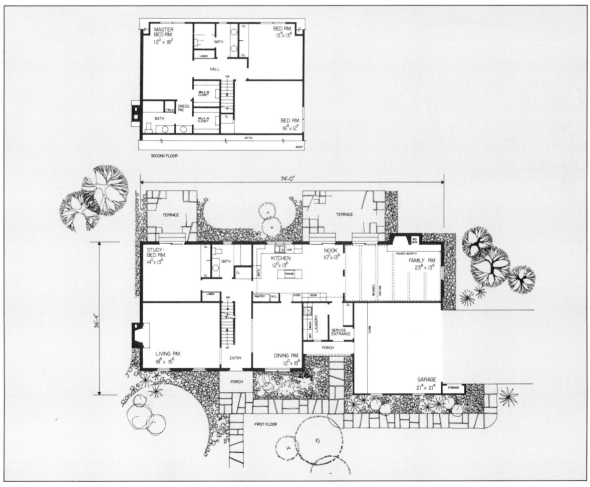

First floor:

896 square feet

Second floor:

1,148 square feet

In this compact Cape, the upper story actually offers more living space than the lower, since the area over the garage has been converted to a generous family room. Access to this versatile room is from the upstairs landing, and the room can be separately zoned for heat and closed off to save energy if desired. A family room thus set up provides an oasis for teenagers who want to play music and hang out with their friends—yet they are still close enough for parental supervision. Downstairs, the living and dining rooms can be opened to each other permanently with an archway or other aperture. Upstairs, the master bath, lit by a dormer like the bedroom it serves, is reached through a dressing area that is flanked by a pair of long closets. China storage downstairs and linen storage upstairs supplement the closets.

The cozy living room, located near the entry, connects to the dining room.

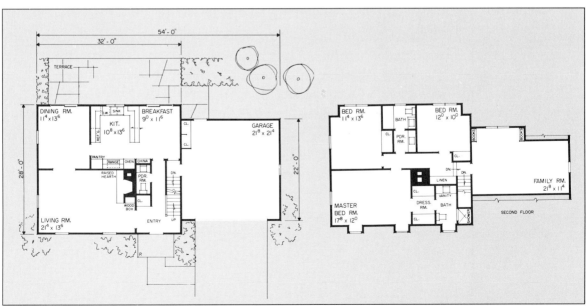

First floor:
1,450 square feet
Second floor:
1,167 square feet

The symmetrical facade of this gambrel Cape, with its trio of dormers, is balanced harmoniously by a narrow laundry wing and commodious garage. Multipaned windows and narrow clapboards unify the exterior. Inside, traffic flows easily from the entry to the dining room and beyond to the U-shaped kitchen, breakfast nook, and family room. The formal living room, by contrast, can be shut off completely for privacy. All rooms upstairs have dormer windows; thus the four bedrooms and two baths are provided with abundant light. For ease of access to the terrace, the family room has two wide, sliding glass doors, a touch that will be appreciated by an active family that really thrives on the outdoors. A truly luxurious addition to the terrace would be a pool! At the other end of the house another exit is located just off the laundry room. There is a full closet here, too, to store boots and other outdoor gear. The laundry room boasts a long counter for sorting clothes; adjacent to it is the pantry—convenient to the kitchen but out of the way of traffic.

The kitchen opens onto the breakfast nook and a gracious bay window overlooking the terrace.

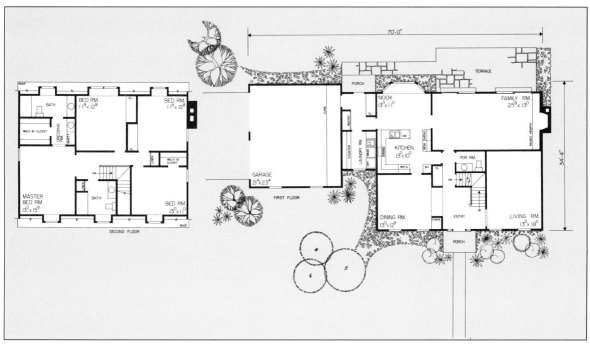

First floor:
1,728 square feet
Second floor:
1,335 square feet

The shingle cladding of this full Cape recalls materials favored by our Colonial ancestors. For contemporary lifestyles, though, the actual design of the house has been altered by an elongated gable at the rear second story and by sliding glass doors. Together, these modifications assure an abundance of light within. The wide entry opens to a living room to the left of the front door and to a more informal family room to the right. The chimney is shared by both the living room and the breakfast room extension of the kitchen. In the kitchen, a large cooking island is an efficient design touch, making it easy to serve breakfast and buffets right from the cooktop. A covered porch links the laundry and the garage. The garage features a second door into the house, accessing a service hall that passes the pantry. All bedrooms have ample closet space attached; the two upstairs baths are spacious and bright. A gigantic corner fireplace in the master suite (stacked over the one in the living room) beckons parents to relax and reflect on their everyday activities long after children have turned in. What a hideaway this suite is—a true tension-relieving oasis.

A large corner fireplace is a unique feature in this master bedroom suite.

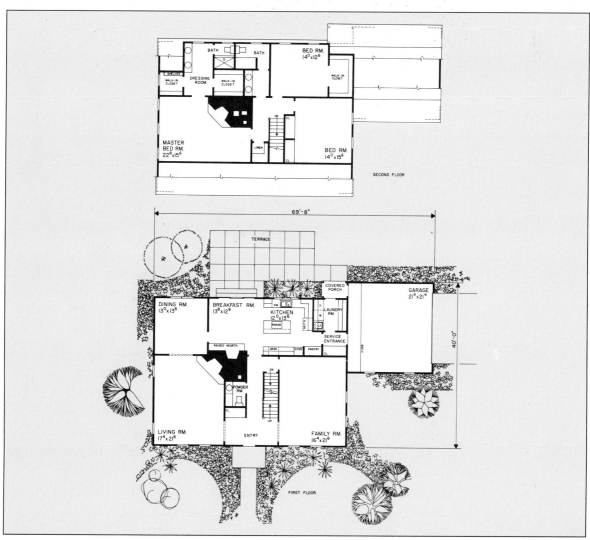

BATH   BATH

DRESSING ROOM

BED RM.
14⁰x12⁶

WALK-IN CLOSET

WALK-IN CLOSET

WALK-IN CLOSET

SHELVES

DW   CL.

MASTER BED RM.
22⁸x15⁶

LINEN

CL.

BED RM.
14⁰x15⁶

SECOND FLOOR

69'-8"

TERRACE

COVERED PORCH

GARAGE
21⁴x21⁴

DINING RM.
13⁰x13⁶

BREAKFAST RM.
13⁸x12⁶

KITCHEN
12⁰x13⁶

RANGE

DW

LAUNDRY RM.

SERVICE ENTRANCE

40'-0"

RAISED HEARTH

DESK   OVEN   PANTRY   CL.

POWDER RM.

CL.

DN

UP

LIVING RM.
17⁴x21⁶

ENTRY

FAMILY RM.
16⁴x21⁶

FIRST FLOOR

89

First floor:
893 square feet
Second floor:
652 square feet

In this gambrel-roofed Cape, the chimney has been positioned at the end of the house to free up more space within. In place of a center chimney, the dwelling is anchored by a wide center hall that leads to all areas of the house with equal ease. A screened porch is an appealing addition, since it can be used both for relaxing and for dining during the warm-weather months. The porch has access to both the kitchen area and to the terraces and lawn. And, for little children who'd love to camp out but don't dare go too far, what a perfect spot to set up an overnight sleep-out! A cozy study at the front of the house affords a pleasant hideaway for reading, complete with built-in bookcase. Two dormered bedrooms, each with its own bath, complete the plan. A picket fence is suggested to enclose the front garden.

The living room, with its fireplace located on the exterior wall, is connected to the dining room.

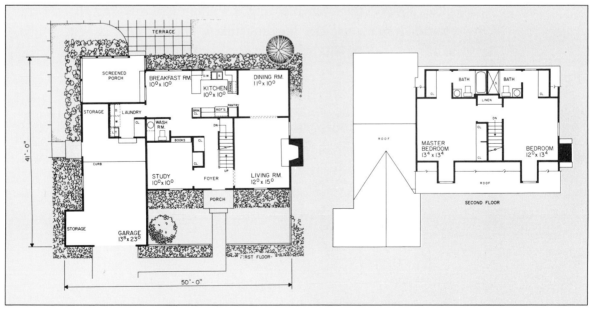

First floor:
1,214 square feet
Second floor:
1,097 square feet

An added bonus of this gambrel-roofed Cape is its extra bedroom located above the family room. This bedroom can be converted to a playroom for an active horde of children and their pals; since it is close to the stairs that lead down to the kitchen area, it is within earshot during play if the door is left ajar. (By the same token, with the door closed, the room can be shut off to become a private study.) The convenient covered porch leads from the driveway directly into the family room and sports two storage nooks built in to stash outdoor gear. The family room adjoins the breakfast nook, and a handy pantry serves both rooms plus the kitchen. A sliding door separates the kitchen from the dining room. A dovecote, weathervane, and barn-door hinges add decorative touches and distinguish the exterior of the attached garage.

The breakfast nook steps down into a family room that contains a fireplace and beamed ceiling.

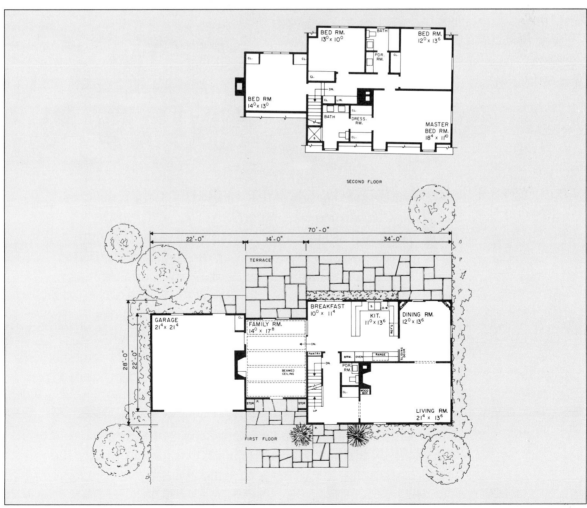

SECOND FLOOR

FIRST FLOOR

First floor:
1,385 square feet
Second floor:
982 square feet

The balanced facade of this shingled full Cape is matched by the harmonious proportions of the living spaces within. The large foyer soars upward to the upstairs center hallway. From the foyer, the view is unobstructed back through the country kitchen and its bay window to the terrace and yard. The kitchen focuses all the various activities of family life; the parents can be preparing dinner while the children cluster at the counter to chat or do homework under their watchful eyes. A screened porch can be reached from both the living room and kitchen. The master suite upstairs has two vanities, one in the dressing room and one in the actual bathroom. Another huge bath serves the other two upstairs bedrooms. A mudroom and a laundry occupy an extension to the house, with the garage just behind. The garage opens to the back of the house so parking is virtually invisible from the street.

Double glass doors separate the spacious country kitchen from the screened porch.

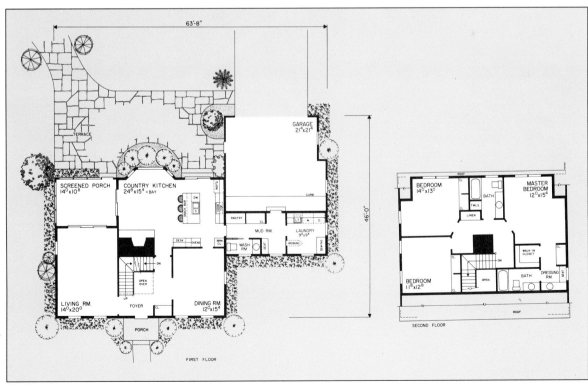

FIRST FLOOR

SECOND FLOOR

Plan B2774, page 102

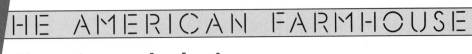

THE AMERICAN FARMHOUSE

Charming and eclectic, our American homestead fits easily into any locale.

First floor:

1,134 square feet

Second floor:

874 square feet

A dramatically angled roofline distinguishes this farm-house, which recalls the vernacular architecture of Texas. Vertical siding is repeated on the trio of gables; the straight lines are echoed in the balustrade wrapping the front porch. Inside, just beyond the entrance, a powder room and laundry occupy the front right corner of the house close to the attached garage and convenient to the service hall, which passes these areas on the way to the family room and actual front entrance. The formal living room to the left of the entry leads directly into the dining room behind. There are, in fact, no doors at all downstairs—although doors can be installed, if desired. Upstairs there are three bedrooms. The large master bedroom has two closets: one a deep walk-in closet, the other a smaller closet.

An ample bay
window overlooks
the backyard from
the dining room.

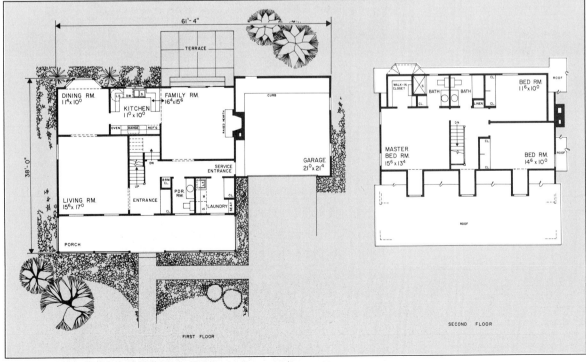

FIRST FLOOR

SECOND FLOOR

First floor:
1,764 square feet
Second floor:
1,506 square feet

The gently sloping gambrel roof of this farmhouse, offset by dentil molding, evokes a Williamsburg design. Porches front and back yield shaded areas for entertaining or just relaxing during warmer months. In addition, the house is raised over an airspace enclosed by a latticed grill to aid in ventilation under the structure—a good precaution against heat and moisture buildup in hot climates. In Northern states, the lattice can be filled in with brick or stone. This house boasts three separate chimneys. The pass-through between the kitchen and the eating area in the family room is sufficiently wide for use as an extra dining surface; serving is a delight from this counter, too, as the cooktop is located here. The master bedroom upstairs has an especially luxurious bath with a tub set into a massive tile surround; a heat lamp can be installed overhead for relaxed stretching out after bathing.

One of the four upstairs bedrooms contains an arched window set into the exterior wall.

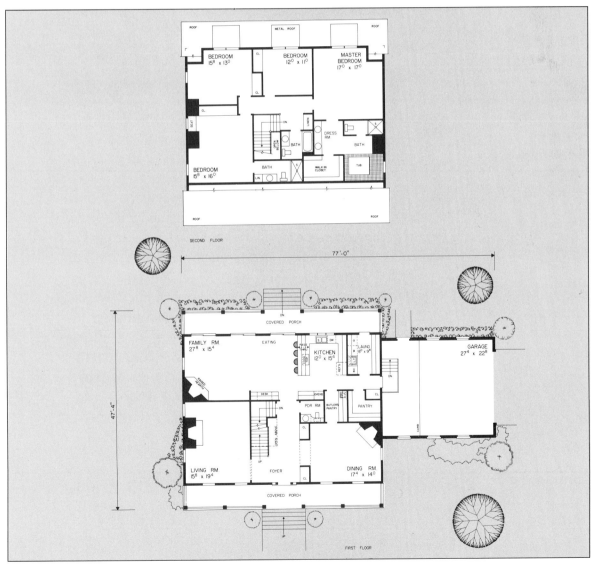

SECOND FLOOR

FIRST FLOOR

First floor:
1,370 square feet
Second floor:
969 square feet

This compact farmhouse provides two—and potentially three—stories for comfortable living. The attic area, in fact, is a huge space with windows at either end that could be enlarged to let in more light. Walls could be dropped down with storage areas tucked behind them under the eaves. On the ground floor, the family room, breakfast room, and kitchen form one unbroken space, much like the keeping rooms of yore. By contrast, the dining room and living room are more formal and private. The garage, reached from a side drive, could open to the porch if desired; as it is, it leads into the house through the laundry and has two big closets just inside the back entry that can hold outdoor gear and work supplies. Both the laundry room and the family room actually step down from the rest of the house. On the second story, three of the four bedrooms share a large bath. The master suite has its own bath, plus a dressing room and three closets.

A raised-hearth fireplace is located on one wall of the family room, alongside a pair of glass doors that lead onto the terrace.

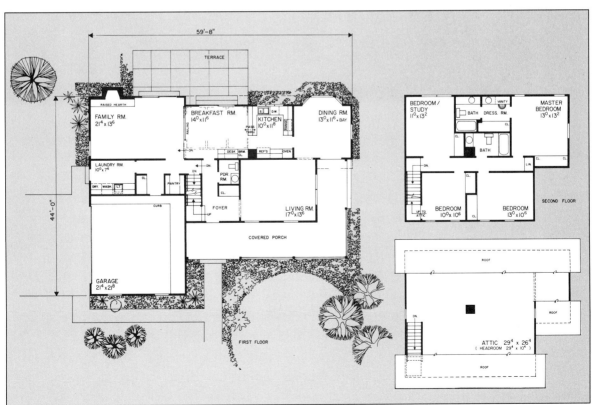

FIRST FLOOR

59'-8"

44'-0"

TERRACE

RAISED HEARTH

FAMILY RM.
21⁴ x 13⁶

BREAKFAST RM.
14⁰ x 11⁶

KITCHEN
10⁰ x 11⁸

DINING RM.
13⁰ x 11⁶ + BAY

LAUNDRY RM.
10⁰ x 7⁶

DESK RM. REF'G OVEN

DRY. WASH CL. PANTRY

PDR. RM.

FOYER

LIVING RM.
17⁰ x 13⁶

CURB

UP

COVERED PORCH

GARAGE
21⁴ x 21⁸

SECOND FLOOR

BEDROOM / STUDY
11⁰ x 13²

BATH DRESS. RM.

VANITY

MASTER BEDROOM
13⁰ x 13²

BATH

DN.

LIN.

UP TO ATTIC

BEDROOM
10⁰ x 10⁶

BEDROOM
13⁰ x 10⁶

ROOF

ROOF

DN.

ATTIC 29⁴ x 26⁴
(HEADROOM 29⁴ x 10⁴)

ROOF

First floor:
2,026 square feet
Second floor:
1,386 square feet

Many early farmhouses grew as the family grew—more children, another wing! This American Federal–style farmhouse recalls this design heritage with its jogs and additions. Besides the typical living spaces expected in a house of this type, there are surprises: a great clutter room that accommodates a tool bench, sewing center, sorting counter, and freezer; and a music alcove, complete with stereo center, off the living room. A grand and graceful staircase leads up through the house. In the master suite, the dressing room is fitted with two window seats that beckon mother and father to rest after a long day. The dressing room can be fitted with exercise equipment—which would prove that the whirlpool bath is more of a necessity than a luxury. After all, a real workout calls for a water massage afterwards!

A window wall in
the farm dining
room looks out onto
the back porch.

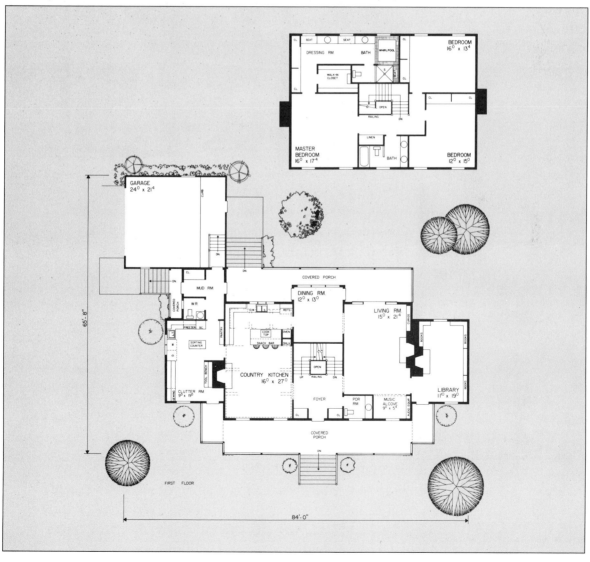

FIRST FLOOR

First floor:
1,308 square feet
Second floor:
1,262 square feet

A double porch extending the length of this farmhouse recalls its antebellum Southern antecedents. The lower porch and its companion upper covered balcony are braced by six handsome columns. A fence linking the upper columns provides not only a gracious architectural accent but, in practical terms, a safe enclosure for adults and children. The house is centered by a spacious foyer leading back to a generous country kitchen. The kitchen is flanked by a formal dining room on one side and a casual built-in bar and laundry on the other. In the kitchen, the cooktop island functions not only as the locus for preparing foods, but as a serving center for the adjacent informal eating area near the kitchen fireplace. Upstairs, the master bedroom is virtually doubled in size by its private dressing room, bath, and walk-in closet. The dressing room has an unusual angled vanity counter buttressed by a linen closet and a cozy window seat. The walk-in closet has a separate area set aside for shoe storage. The other three bedrooms on this floor share a large bath with an extra vanity, and they also share a linen closet conveniently located near all three rooms.

The cozy living room, with its built-in fireplace, is connected to the dining room by an open entrance wall.

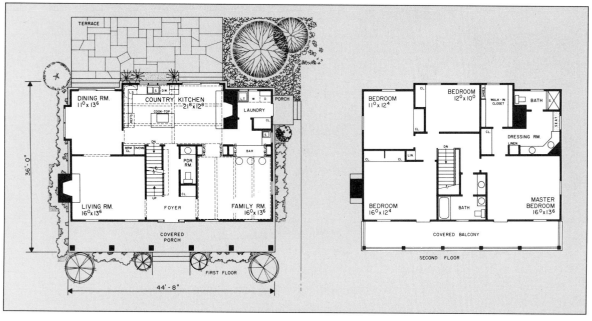

First floor:
1,451 square feet
Second floor:
1,091 square feet

One of the special features of this appealing farmhouse is the stacked configuration of fireplaces; in other words, the plan displays not only the traditional fireplace in the gathering room, but also another fireplace upstairs in the master bedroom. The master bedroom is rendered even more special by its two dormer windows and a step-into dressing room-closet-bath suite. The linen area at the top of the stairs is lighted by a dormer. Downstairs, the gathering room pulls in daylight on three sides; the far wall, in fact, is almost all glass due to its triple-width sliding glass door. The gathering room is completely open to the dining room, just as the kitchen is open to the breakfast nook: This is a house geared to informal living on a generous scale.

The dormer windows and built-in fireplace are unique features of the master bedroom.

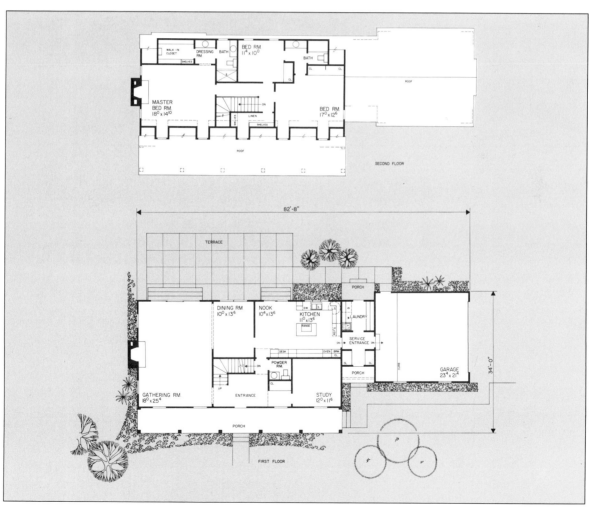

First floor:

1,317 square feet

Second floor:

952 square feet

A wraparound porch distinguishes this farmhouse and provides plenty of shade during summertime—or during the entire year if the house is built in the Sunbelt. Upstairs windows are set back and shaded by a deep roof overhang. The twin front windows in the living room could be converted to French doors, perfect for letting in breezes. Conversely, during colder spells, the fireplace is a welcome addition to the family room. The dining room could open directly to the breakfast nook for a more spacious feeling, especially for a family that prefers informal living throughout the house. Four bedrooms upstairs offer the option of setting aside a special room for guests who stay overnight.

T he glass doors and large windows in the living room look out onto the wrap-around covered porch.

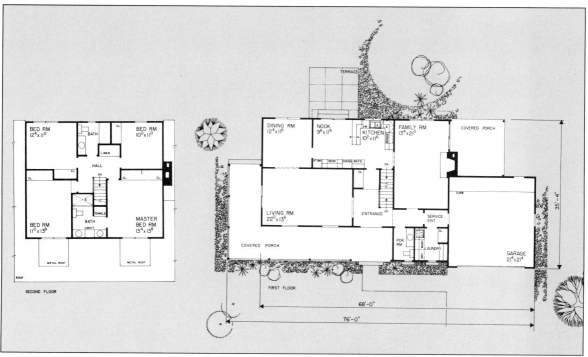

SECOND FLOOR

BED RM.
12⁴x11⁰

BATH

CL

BED RM.
10⁰x11⁰

LINEN

HALL

CL

CL

CL

CL

DN

BED RM.
11⁰x13⁸

BATH

TOWELS

VANITY

MASTER
BED RM
13⁴x13⁸

METAL ROOF

METAL ROOF

ROOF

FIRST FLOOR

TERRACE

DINING RM.
12⁴x13⁶

NOOK
9⁶x11⁶

KITCHEN
10²x11⁶

FAMILY RM.
13⁴x21⁰

COVERED PORCH

PNTRY DESK OVENS REF'E

CL

DN

LIVING RM.
22⁰x13⁶

ENTRANCE UP

SERVICE
ENT.

CURB

COVERED PORCH

PDR
RM

WASH

CL

LAUNDRY

GARAGE
21⁴x21⁴

68'-0"

76'-0"

35'-4"

111

First floor:
1,350 square feet
Second floor:
1,224 square feet

Greek Revival features, such as pilasters and rudimentary capitals replacing corner boards, lend immediate appeal to the facade of this farmhouse. The actual structure is an L embracing a cozy covered porch, with a garage added on. Access to the front porch is through French doors from the living room. This room, and the dining room behind, are anchored by a massive raised hearth and fireplace opening in both directions to both rooms. The mudroom steps down from the dining room and links it to the garage; there is a washroom here, too. The master suite is grand, with its large dressing room and a separate "secret" storage nook hidden behind the master bedroom. Two additional bedrooms share a bath and tuck under the eaves.

A large, raised-hearth fireplace opens onto both the dining and family rooms.

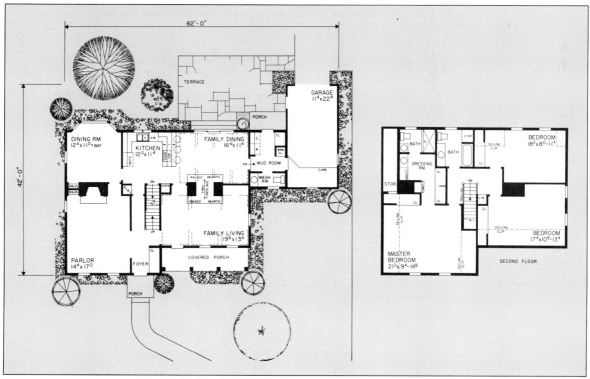

62'-0"

42'-0"

DINING RM.
12⁴x11⁰+BAY

KITCHEN
12⁰x11⁴

TERRACE

GARAGE
11⁴x22⁴

PORCH

FAMILY DINING
16⁴x11⁴

MUD ROOM

WASH RM

RAISED   HEARTH

THRU FIREPLACE

RAISED   HEARTH

FAMILY LIVING
19⁸x13⁴

PARLOR
14⁴x17⁰

FOYER

COVERED PORCH

PORCH

BATH

DRESSING RM

STOR

STOR

BATH

CEILING CLIP

BEDROOM
18²x8⁰-11⁴

TOWELS

MASTER
BEDROOM
21⁰9⁴-14⁸

CEILING CLIP

BEDROOM
17⁴x10⁸-13⁴

SECOND FLOOR

First floor:
1,707 square feet
Second floor:
1,439 square feet

The curved-gambrel roofline typical of early Dutch Colonial
dwellings hugs the upper story of this charming farmhouse and then flares out to cover generous porches at the
front and rear of the structure. Three dormers pierce the
front roof and are subtly rounded to echo the sweep of the roof
itself. The house is bracketed by a pair of chimneys. Inside, one
fireplace warms the big country kitchen while, at the opposite
end of the house, a pair of back-to-back corner fireplaces lends a
cozy note to the living room and to the study next door. The
dining room protrudes from the back of the house, flanked by a
covered porch on either side. Entertaining is a delight on these
porches; in warm months guests can step down to a full terrace
beyond. The second story has three bedrooms and two baths—
but there is also a fourth bedroom, with its own bath, situated
over the garage. This bedroom, reached also by a back staircase,
can be zoned as an apartment or office, or it can be used as a
guest suite, or, in a big family, as the master suite.

A spacious open area combines the country kitchen and beamed-ceiling family room.

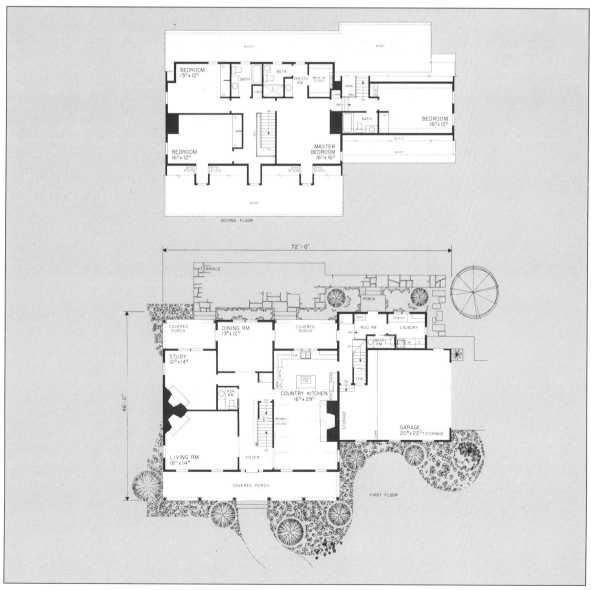

SECOND FLOOR

BEDROOM
13⁰ x 12⁰

BATH

DRESS'G RM

WALK IN CLOSET

BATH

BEDROOM
16⁰ x 12⁰

BEDROOM
16⁰ x 12⁰

MASTER BEDROOM
16⁰ x 16⁰

BATH

ATTIC ACCESS

72'-0"

46'-0"

TERRACE

PORCH

COVERED PORCH

DINING RM
13⁸ x 12⁰

COVERED PORCH

MUD RM

LAUNDRY

WASH RM

STUDY
12⁸ x 14⁴

PDR RM

COUNTRY KITCHEN
16⁰ x 29⁰

STORAGE

GARAGE
20⁸ x 22⁰+STORAGE

LIVING RM
18⁰ x 14⁴

BEAMED CEILING

FOYER

COVERED PORCH

FIRST FLOOR

First floor:
1,612 square feet

Second floor:
1,356 square feet

If you removed the porch from this farmhouse, it would recall its Cape Cod forebears. The porch is a welcome respite from summer's heat and offers protection from rain and snow. Five gables enhance the roof and provide bonus nooks for two upstairs bedrooms. The foyer leads easily to the formal areas at the front of the house, and to the informal areas at the back. A special added touch is the "tavern" just off the back hall, which extends from the family room. The compact U-shaped kitchen serves many eating areas: the dining room, the breakfast area in the family room, and the tavern. A covered porch on the back of the house can also be used for dining—even for barbecuing in inclement weather. Upstairs, the master suite is a sybaritic paradise for an overworked mom and dad. Imagine bathing in its grand, overscaled tub, perhaps a whirlpool!

The comfortable family room contains a beamed ceiling, a raised-hearth fireplace, and a spacious bay window overlooking the backyard.

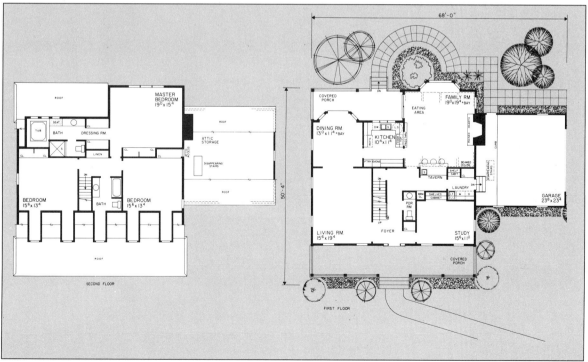

SECOND FLOOR

FIRST FLOOR

First floor:
2,025 square feet
Second floor:
1,726 square feet

Although this classic farmhouse is sheathed in fieldstone, the exterior can be adapted to brick or wood. Fieldstone is indigenous to Pennsylvania and evokes the design traditions of our Pennsylvania Dutch ancestors. Paneled shutters on the lower windows of the house offset the rugged stone; shutters can be added to all windows, if desired. One hallmark of the interior is the number of fireplaces—five in all. Three of these share one chimney and the other two the second. The family room is particularly luxurious in scale and sports a unique arrangement of ceiling beams. A woodbox with bookcase above finishes off the fireplace wall. In the kitchen, the range is set into a chimney block and a work island supplements countertops as a preparation surface. The master bedroom above the family room has its own fireplace—and two walk-in closets, one for him and one for her. The other three bedrooms share a lounge, stair landing, and a bath with two vanities.

The cozy corner of the beamed family room contains built-in bookcases, a raised-hearth fireplace, and a step-in pantry.

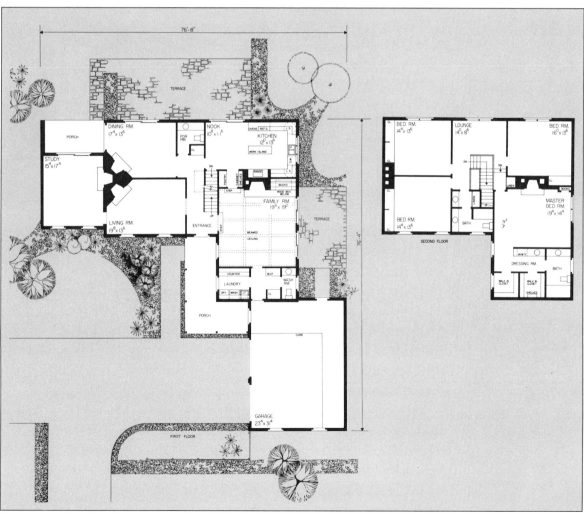

First floor:
1,338 square feet
Second floor:
1,200 square feet
Third floor:
506 square feet

This brick-faced farmhouse in the Georgian style is reminiscent of farmsteads traditional to the Pennsylvania Dutch countryside. The symmetry of the structure is offset and dramatized by the simple, sturdy front porch. The utility wing and garage extension to the house are accented by a roof overhang based on an authentic Pennsylvania pent-roof design. The harmony of the exterior is reflected inside. The living room, for example, matches the opposed beamed family room in size and scale. The same is true of the dining room and study. Both the living and family rooms feature impressive corner fireplaces that serve as the focal point of each space. The bonus of this plan is the third story, with two spaces that can be used for hobbies or study, or for guest quarters or extra children's rooms. These rooms share a bath on the second story with three bedrooms, but a bath (or two) could be tucked in under the eaves if desired by following the plumbing lines. The ample master suite features a dressing room and private bath.

The farm kitchen overlooks the family room, offering a view of the corner fireplace.

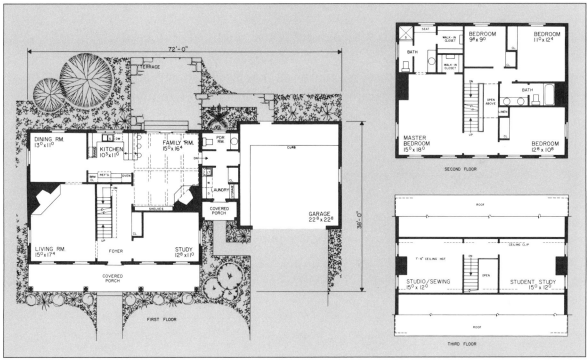

FIRST FLOOR

72'-0"

TERRACE

DINING RM.
13⁰ x 11⁰

KITCHEN
10³ x 11⁰

FAMILY RM.
15⁰ x 16⁴

PDR RM.

REF'S   OVEN

LAUNDRY

SHELVES

COVERED PORCH

CURB

GARAGE
22⁸ x 22⁸

38'-0"

LIVING RM.
15⁰ x 17⁴

FOYER

STUDY
12⁸ x 11⁰

COVERED PORCH

SECOND FLOOR

SEAT

BATH

WALK-IN CLOSET

BEDROOM
9⁸ x 9⁰

BEDROOM
11⁰ x 12⁴

WALK-IN CLOSET

CL

DN

OPEN ABOVE

BATH

LINEN

UP

CL

MASTER BEDROOM
15⁰ x 18⁰

BEDROOM
12⁸ x 10⁸

THIRD FLOOR

ROOF

CEILING CLIP

7'-6" CEILING HGT.

DN

OPEN

STUDIO/SEWING
15⁰ x 12⁰

STUDENT STUDY
15⁰ x 12⁰

ROOF

First floor:
1,266 square feet
Second floor:
1,232 square feet

This traditional farmhouse, sheathed in stone and clapboards, is braced by two chimneys and accented by a narrow, covered front porch. The square entrance hall leads directly into a huge living room running the depth of the house; a rounded bay window in this room looks out to the front yard. The efficient U-shaped kitchen serves the breakfast nook and more formal dining room with equal ease. Upstairs are five bedrooms, perfect for a larger family. One or more of these rooms, though, could be set apart to use as a crafts space, or room for music, reading, or just play. The master bath incorporates a seat in its shower stall.

The beamed-ceiling family room, containing a raised-hearth fireplace, is illuminated by sunlight from the two large windows.

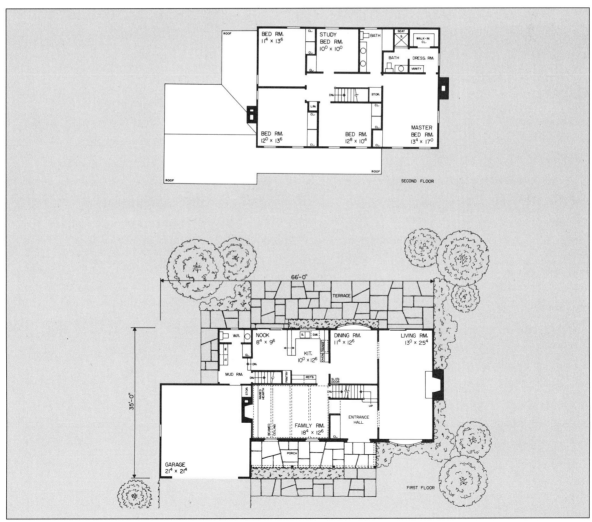

Single level:
1,515 square feet

For a compact farmhouse-style home, this plan offers an
enormous amount of open-plan space in combination
with generous private areas and plenty of storage besides.
The gathering room combines living and dining, a boon
for a couple who relish entertaining. This room steps down to a
large terrace, which leads around a flower bed to the master
bedroom. In the breakfast nook, a pantry wall can be converted
to open storage for display of treasured dinnerware or collectibles. The recessed entry offers respite from nasty weather and
ensures a modicum of shade when it is very hot outdoors. A nod
to the Greek Revival style is evident in the pilasters and corner
detailing on the bedroom and garage wing.

The spacious gathering room offers generous space for living and for dining.

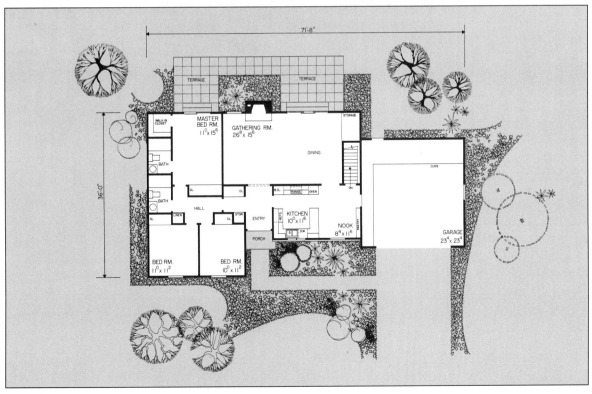

First floor:
1,506 square feet
Second floor:
1,156 square feet

Building this brick-faced farmhouse on an L enhances its convenience, as every major room branches neatly and logically off the main entry. Only a separate bedroom, cut off for privacy so that it can accommodate guests or be used as a study, is not immediately connected to the foyer. The wall between the living room and this study could come down to almost double the living room area, if desired. The laundry and an adjacent bath act as a buffer zone between the bedroom-study and the kitchen with its breakfast alcove. Upstairs rooms have a slight setback at the corners; the baths and one bedroom extend into a gabled zone. Over the family room is a lounge area reserved for parents who want a private hideaway. This lounge opens into a huge storage attic over the garage. A spiral stair could be installed in the garage to lead up to the attic; this space could then be devoted to a play area for children.

The raised-hearth fireplace in the family room is flanked by two doors. The door on the left leads to the garage, the door on the right opens to a wood box.

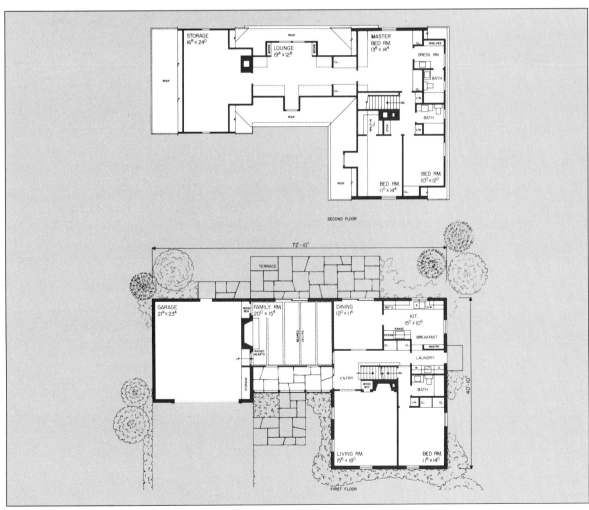

STORAGE
16⁸ x 24⁰

ROOF

LOUNGE
19⁴ x 12⁸

MASTER
BED RM.
13⁸ x 14⁴

SHELVES

DRESS. RM.

BATH

ROOF

CL.

CL.

ON.

BATH

LIN.

WALK-IN
CL.

STOR.

LIN.

BED RM.
10⁰ x 12⁰

ROOF

ROOF

BED RM.
11⁰ x 14⁴

CL.

SECOND FLOOR

72'-10"

TERRACE

GARAGE
21⁴ x 23⁴

WOOD
BOX

FAMILY RM.
20⁰ x 15⁴

BEAMED
CEILING

DINING
12⁰ x 11⁶

REF'S.

S

KIT.
15⁰ x 10⁶

D.W.

RAISED
HEARTH

RANGE

OVENS

CL.

BREAKFAST

PANTRY

STORAGE

UP

LAUNDRY

W

D

ENTRY

DN.

WOOD
BOX

BATH

40'-10"

LIN.

CL.

LIVING RM.
15⁶ x 18⁰

BED RM.
11⁶ x 14⁰

FIRST FLOOR

127

Single level:
2,889 square feet

One-floor living, farmhouse style, is appealing to anyone who dislikes climbing stairs, and especially retirees who are consolidating their living arrangements. Certain zones in this stylish house, specifically the two front bedrooms, can be closed off without affecting the traffic patterns throughout the house. The master bedroom and an adjacent study comprise another private living zone. The central focus of the house—but one that can be zoned off, too—is a grand gathering room with sloped ceiling. This room is perfect for entertaining indoors or out, as twin pairs of sliding glass doors lead to the terrace. Inside, a huge fireplace dominates this impressive central area. Intimate, formal dining takes place in a dining room near the kitchen, and there is a breakfast nook besides. The laundry makes room for an upright freezer that can store quantities of foods close to the kitchen, but out of its way.

In the spacious gathering room, the sloped ceiling permits glass doors and clerestory windows on either side of the raised-hearth fireplace.

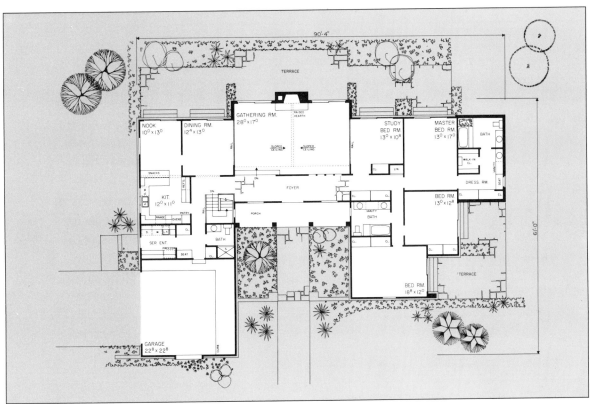

First floor:
1,701 square feet
Second floor:
1,340 square feet

The versatility of this farmhouse is indicated at once by the fact that it incorporates a large, separate suite over the family room. This suite, as indicated, can be reserved for guests, but it also could—just as easily—be devoted to a teenager, to a live-in relative, or to the parents of the household. In the latter instance, it is recommended that a doorway be introduced between the two closets to the actual master bedroom and that this suite be used as a home office or project area. Downstairs, the heart of the house is the family room with its beamed ceiling and fireplace. Another fireplace, with a woodbox, highlights the living room; this room could be turned into a den or library. Outside, the pleasing brick is offset by clapboards and a dovecote.

Stairs to the guest suite are located at one end of the large family room.

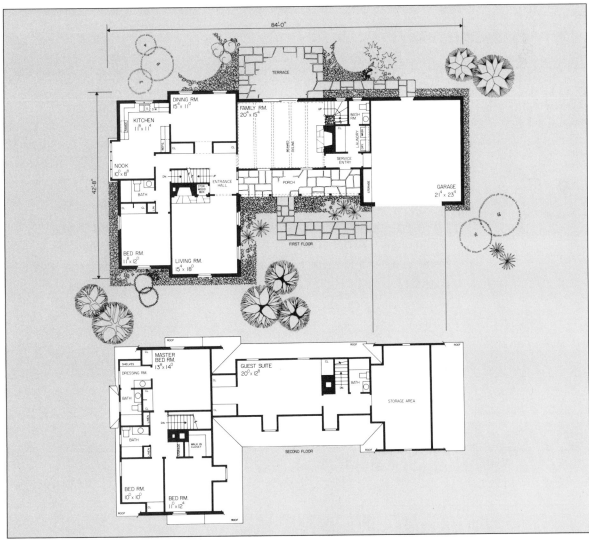

84'-0"

42'-8"

TERRACE

DINING RM.
15⁴ x 11⁰

KITCHEN
11⁸ x 11⁴

FAMILY RM.
20⁰ x 15⁴

WASH RM.

LAUNDRY

NOOK
10⁰ x 8⁸

BATH

ENTRANCE HALL

STOR. WOOD BOX

SERVICE ENTRY

BED RM.
11⁸ x 12⁰

LIVING RM.
15⁴ x 18⁰

PORCH

STORAGE

GARAGE
21⁴ x 23⁴

FIRST FLOOR

ROOF

SHELVES

MASTER BED RM.
13⁸ x 14⁰

DRESSING RM.

BATH

BATH

GUEST SUITE
20⁰ x 12⁸

BATH

STORAGE AREA

ROOF

ROOF

DN

WALK IN CLOSET

BED RM.
10⁰ x 10⁰

BED RM.
11⁸ x 12⁴

SECOND FLOOR

ROOF

ROOF

ROOF

131

Single level:

1,936 square feet

As a single-story structure, this farmhouse steps back, in stages, from a garage to a center core to a bedroom wing. Yet all stepbacks are visually unified by narrow clapboards, shingled roof, and an appealing covered porch. The tiled entry hall leads past the family room, with its open-colonnaded wall, to a step-down living room. To the right of the entry are the kitchen, a substantial nook for casual dining, and a convenient powder room. A buffet and china cabinet accent the nook. Two of the three bedrooms in the wing share a bath; the master bedroom claims its own private bath. Two separate back terraces complete the plan.

The U-shaped kitchen is connected to the breakfast nook on one side, the dining room on the other.

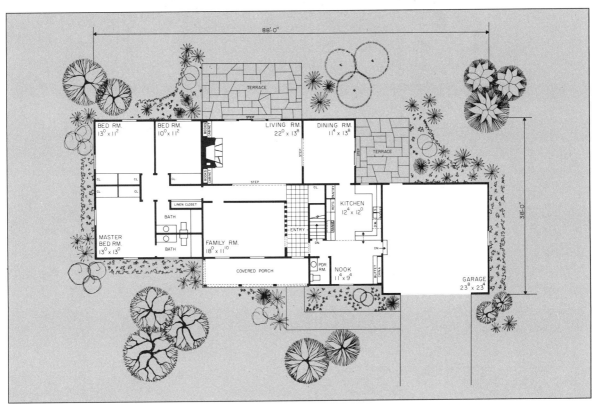

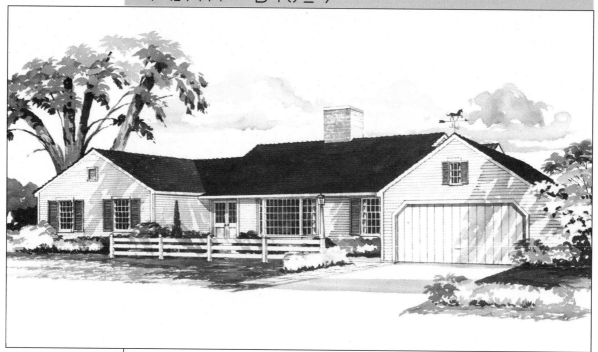

Single level:

1,800 square feet

The enduring appeal of this farmhouse is evident from the street: Big multipaned windows, including a huge bay window to the living room, and an entrance court defined by a casual fence are sure clues to the charm of this dwelling. Because the house is so compact, not an inch is wasted. The garage, in fact, gives over some of its space not only to extra storage, but also to a full laundry and adjacent powder room. The kitchen, an efficient U-shape, has a convenient pass-through to the breakfast nook. The fireplace cavity awaits an energy-efficient woodstove. There are four bedrooms in the house, but each pair—the two front bedrooms and the master bedroom and room adjacent—could be exploded to create two large bedrooms. This option is perfect for retirees or "empty-nesters" who long for extra space and fewer bedrooms.

The family room, adjacent to the U-shaped kitchen, contains a raised-hearth fireplace.

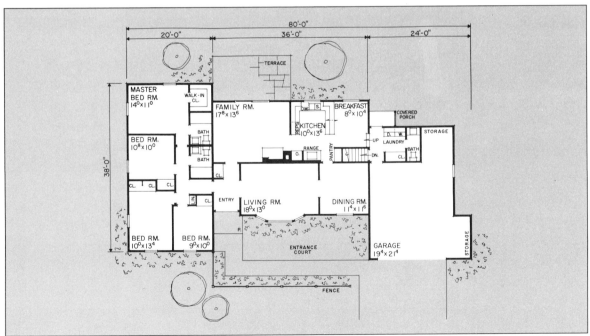

First floor:
1,851 square feet
Second floor:
762 square feet

Long and low in its appearance, this farmhouse actually bumps up to a second story over the main body of the structure. Upstairs rooms in this section face the backyard for privacy, with ancillary storage areas tucked in under the roof at the front of the house. Board-and-batten siding lends visual height to the facade and is married to neat brick on the living room wing to the left of the foyer. In this house, parents have their private domain on the ground floor, through a bath to the right of the foyer. This bath could be closed off completely as there is a secondary washroom off the family room, which would more likely be the center of any entertaining. The plan provides plenty of storage throughout the house, and porches both front and rear.

One entire wall of the family room contains a large, deeply set bay window.

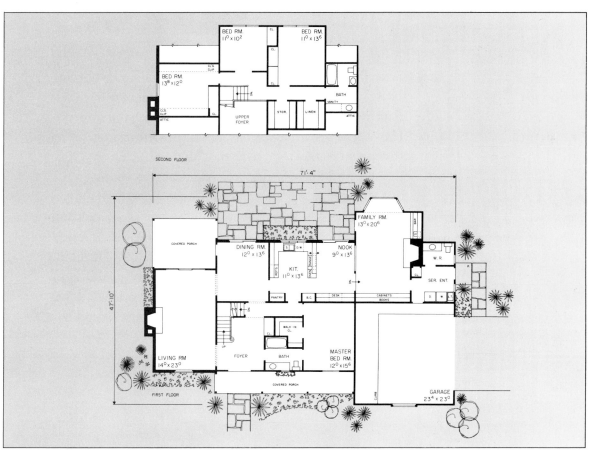

First floor:

990 square feet

Second floor:

728 square feet

An excellent starter house, this dwelling offers two options for its second story: bedrooms and baths change from one plan, with four bedrooms, to the other, with only three. The overall square footage is identical. One or more of the bedrooms could be converted to a study and hobby room. One bedroom, too, could be reserved as a playroom for young children. Downstairs, the garage leads directly into the family room, which, though it steps down from the breakfast nook and kitchen, looks into these spaces over a railing. The raised hearth in the family room is a cozy focus for many activities. The living room has a huge multipaned window that pulls in available light under a covered porch—a boon since there are no side windows. Because of the window placement, in fact, this house would be a logical choice for a tight building spot.

The living room, with its ample entrance from the foyer, contains a large window overlooking the front porch.

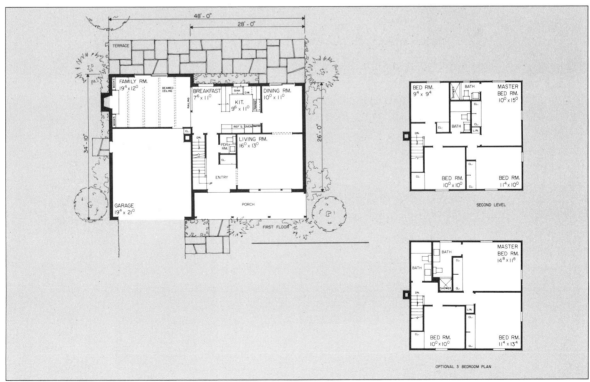

Single level:
2,392 square feet

This eye-catching farmhouse combines traditional exterior detailing with all the convenient aspects of today's best home designs. The board-and-batten siding and stones are materials associated with Old World farmhouses, as are the dovecote and gaslight. Inside, however, the plan is dedicated to modern efficiency. The spacious foyer steps down to the grand gathering room with its sloping ceiling and massive fireplace. Two sets of sliding glass doors lead to the terrace. The private areas of the house—the four bedrooms and two baths—can be zoned for complete privacy. The one linking bath, in fact, can be closed off from the foyer completely. There is a powder room located to the left of the entry that can be used for guests. The kitchen opens naturally to the breakfast room with its huge bay window, and on to the dining room beyond. The dining room leads back to the gathering room, thus completing the traffic circle.

The sloped ceilings in this large gathering room are beamed and glass doors flank the rustic fireplace.

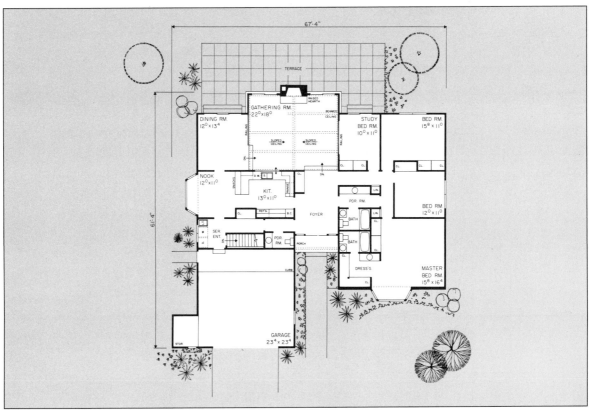

Lower level:
528 square feet

Main level:
871 square feet

Upper level:
1,132 square feet

Billed as a tri-level, this L-shaped farmhouse actually steps down from its formal rooms and kitchen to an informal family room and garage. A level up leads to the bedrooms, which occupy the floor over the family room and garage. The formal living and dining rooms are highlighted by twin bay windows facing the side yard. The breakfast nook and family room both lead to expansive terraces at the back of the house. The covered porch protects the main entrance while a second entrance is located off the garage. In the family room, a raised hearth stretches the entire width of the room—perfect for gathering groups in front of the fire. Upstairs, one front bedroom protrudes beyond the facade to achieve extra space. The master bedroom opens to its own private balcony.

Twin bay windows, in the living and dining rooms, overlook the side yard and fill the rooms with sunlight.

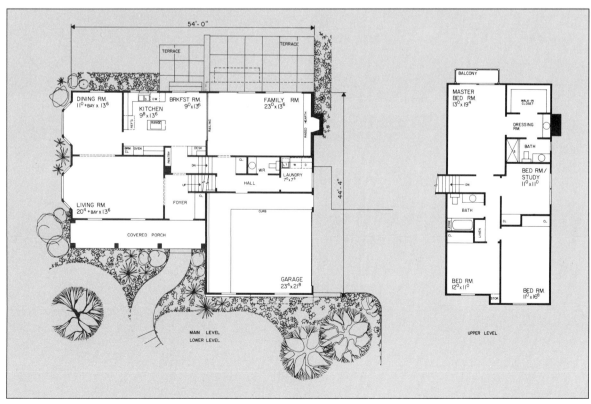

54'- 0"

44'- 4"

TERRACE
TERRACE

DINING RM.
11⁰+BAY x 13⁶

BRKFST RM.
9⁸x13⁶

KITCHEN
9⁸x13⁶

REF'G

DW

RANGE

BRM CL

OVEN

FAMILY RM.
23⁰x13⁶

RAILING

RAISED HEARTH

PANTRY

DESK

DN

CL

W.R.

W

T

D

LAUNDRY
7⁰x7⁶

LIVING RM.
20⁴+BAY x 13⁶

FOYER

UP

HALL

CURB

COVERED PORCH

GARAGE
23⁴x21⁸

MAIN LEVEL
LOWER LEVEL

BALCONY

MASTER
BED RM.
13⁰x19⁴

WALK-IN
CLOSET

DRESSING
RM.

BATH

BED RM./
STUDY
11⁰x11⁰

DN

BATH

LEDGE

CL

LINEN

CL

CL

BED RM.
12⁰x11⁰

STOR.

BED RM.
11⁰x16⁸

UPPER LEVEL

First floor:
2,052 square feet
Second floor:
1,425 square feet

A clever amalgam of materials—board-and-batten siding, stone, and brick—defines the different and specific areas of this farmhouse, while setting up an energetic visual counterpoint of textures on the exterior. The splayed recessed entry is yet another delightful touch. The living room (that's the brick wing!) runs the complete depth of the house, yielding light-gathering windows on three sides. The living room is accessed both from the entry and from the dining room through wide openings; these can be fitted with doors if privacy is desired. The service entrance conducts traffic to the informal areas of the house and features two entries—one from a small second porch to the left of the actual front entry porch. A washroom with shower, and a seat render the service entry particularly useful to children who have played outdoors and to pets that need to be cleaned up and dried off.

A study downstairs, with built-in bookcases and closet, leads to the service entrance of the house.

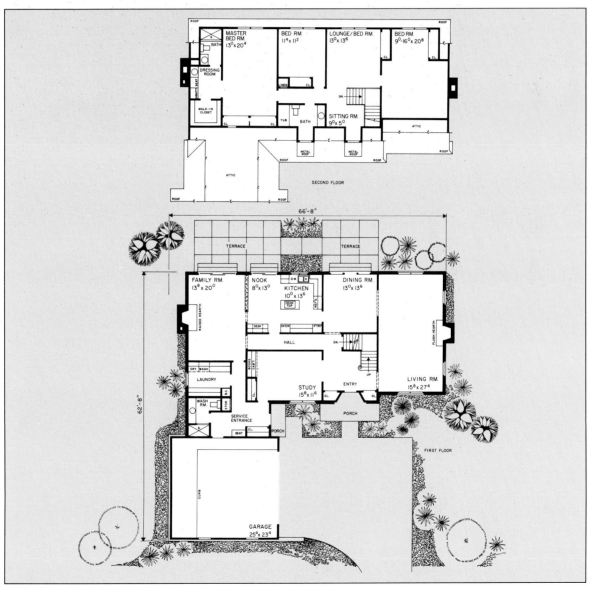

SECOND FLOOR

FIRST FLOOR

Single level:
1,547 square feet

In this single-story farmhouse, the roof covering the rear porch is pierced by a trio of skylights that greatly add to the daylight entering both the porch area and the living and dining rooms that lead off it. This porch can be reached as well from the casual breakfast nook. The combination of TV, study, and bedroom is centrally located as a focus of everyday life. Especially attractive to a retired couple, this room can be handily closed off if either husband or wife enjoys staying up to watch late-night TV! The front bedroom can be reserved for guests or visiting relatives, leaving the area undisturbed. The garage incorporates a large storage zone adjacent to the back entrance to the house. This area also opens to the yard so the zone can be reserved for garden supplies and lawn mower. Notice that the basic plan offers an optional "non-basement" where the central heating and cooling unit can be placed in the space occupied by the basement stairs.

A sloped ceiling runs the entire length—from the dining room to the living room.

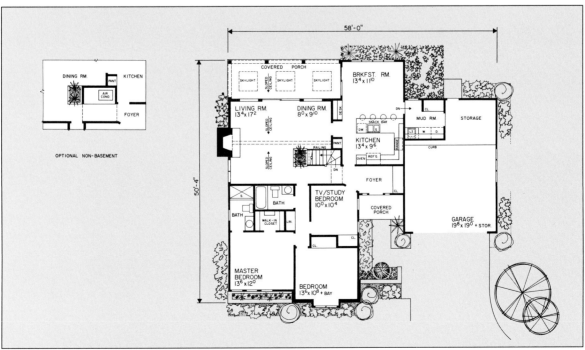

OPTIONAL NON-BASEMENT

Single level:
1,267 square feet

As a starter house or a dwelling for a retired couple, this farmhouse exhibits every convenience within a very compact framework. The living room, dining room, and kitchen all interconnect, one to the next, for an easy-going traffic flow. The kitchen provides a cozy corner for lingering over breakfast or an extra cup of coffee. The master bedroom and living room open to a terrace and the backyard. The bedroom chosen to be converted to a study could move its access from the entry hall around to the bedroom hall so that the room would be more convenient to the bath it shares with the corner bedroom. Instead of stone, the exterior can be sheathed entirely in board-and-batten siding for a more unified effect, if desired.

The eat-in kitchen contains a pass-through to the dining room, which permits a view of the backyard.

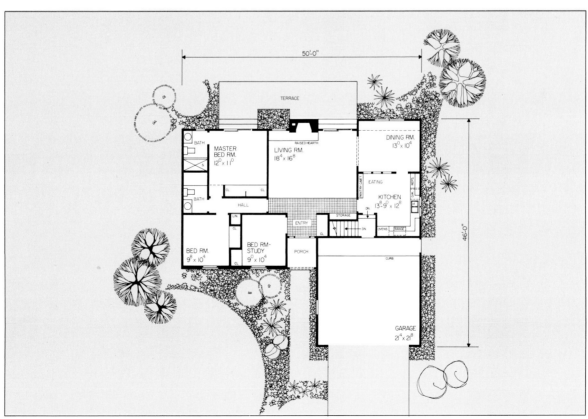

First floor:
1,202 square feet
Second floor:
896 square feet

The compactness of this tidy farmhouse belies its immeasurable liveability! There's a powder room just off the entry that proves handy for guests, and a laundry alongside that doubles as a mudroom for children and pets coming in from the outdoors. The laundry connects the garage to the family room and kitchen beyond. The family room has a beamed ceiling to enhance its coziness. China storage in the kitchen area can be left open to display dinnerware or closed up, as desired. Each of the four bedrooms upstairs occupies a corner location so that each looks out in two directions; this also adds to the ambient light in each room. The mix of materials on the exterior of the farmhouse lends vigor to the overall design. Special accents include the X-braced front door with six-panel sidelights and a cupola with weathervane capping the garage.

Two glass doors on the exterior wall of the cozy dining room look out onto a patio.

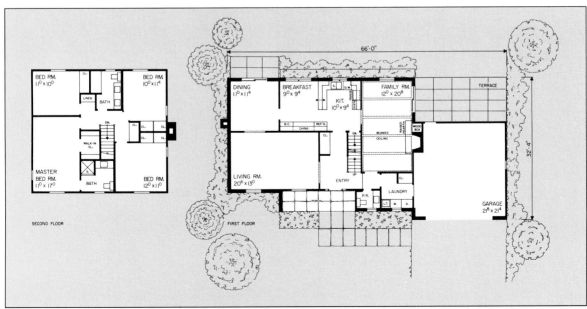

BED RM.
11⁰ x 10⁰

CL.

BED RM.
10⁰ x 11⁴

LINEN

BATH

DN.

CL.

CL.

CL.

CL.

WALK-IN
CL.

MASTER
BED RM.
11⁰ x 17⁰

BATH

BED RM.
12⁰ x 11⁰

SECOND FLOOR

66'-0"

DINING
11⁰ x 11⁴

BREAKFAST
9⁰ x 9⁴

TERRACE

KIT.
10⁰ x 9⁴

FAMILY RM.
12⁰ x 20⁸

B.C.

REF'G.

CHINA

CL.

DN.

BEAMED
CEILING

RAISED
HEARTH

WOOD
BOX

32'-4"

LIVING RM.
20⁶ x 13⁰

UP

ENTRY

CL.

PORCH

P.R.

L.T.

W

D

LAUNDRY

GARAGE
21⁸ x 21⁴

FIRST FLOOR

Plan B2610, page 192

THE CENTER-HALL CLASSIC

Gracious and hospitable, this elegant domain adds dignity to any neighborhood.

First floor:
1,272 square feet
Second floor:
1,139 square feet

The shingled cladding of this center-hall Colonial evokes images of similarly sheathed houses on Cape Cod or Nantucket. The shuttered front doorway is transom-lit. Other windows are calculated to take full advantage of the daylight, especially at the rear of the house, where multipaned glass doors illuminate the family room and the music alcove off the living room. This alcove can convert to a separate, private sitting room—intimate and cozy for reading or for sharing coffee or tea with a special friend. Two fireplaces flare off the center chimney. In the family room, the hearth is raised and can be a close-to-the-fire perch for family and friends alike. A separate entrance at the back of the house leads into the mudroom so yard and garden are instantly accessible, and there is no danger of tracking dirt back into the house. Two linen closets flank a window seat in the upstairs hall—another charming hideaway! Two bedrooms boast dressing room-bath suites. The center bedroom can be used as a lounge or TV room.

The open stairway offers an area for display at the entrance to the house.

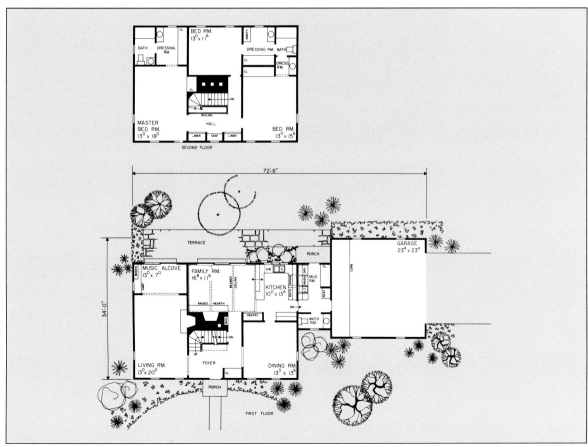

First floor:
1,317 square feet
Second floor:
681 square feet

Based on an early Nantucket lean-to design, this tidy shingled center-hall Colonial, like its antecedent, places its keeping room and kitchen at the back of the house under the lean-to "addition," while the formal rooms and bedrooms occupy the core structure. White-painted Greek Revival–style pilasters and entablature beautify the entrance. Inside, the entrance hall is highlighted by an angular stairwell. Behind rises a massive center chimney containing two fireplaces, one of which is complemented by a bread oven. The kitchen extends into a low-key eating area with a china cabinet notched into one corner to be used for both storage and display. The dead-end bedroom at the front of the ground floor can be opened to the entrance hall, if desired. As a private haven it works wonderfully as a home office for either mother or father—or the room could be enjoyed by the entire family, with the closet given over to a full complement of stereo and television equipment. If this lean-to is used as a starter or "empty-nest" home, one of the upstairs bedrooms can be converted to a lounge or grand dressing room.

The beamed-ceiling keeping room is located at the back of the house, beneath the low, lean-to roof.

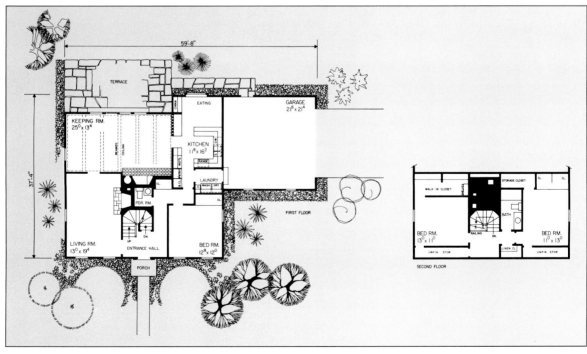

First floor:
1,672 square feet
Second floor:
1,287 square feet

*T*he saltbox roof-pitch of this center-hall Colonial is pierced by a long, high gable so that twin back bedrooms on the second floor are provided with plenty of space and light. The walkway to the house offers visitors two options: the formal entrance, used most probably for formal entertaining; and the mudroom entrance, used most of the time by family, friends, and relatives. In the family room, the fireplace wall is equipped with a woodbox. A storage nook keeps papers and matches for making fires out of the way—a boon in households with young children. The study downstairs converts to a guest room, which is served not only by a powder room but also by a shower. Corner cabinets in the dining room display treasured family china and porcelain. The second story provides organized storage solutions; each closet is subdivided so summer and winter clothes can be separated easily.

The study downstairs, with built-in bookshelves, can substitute for a guest bedroom.

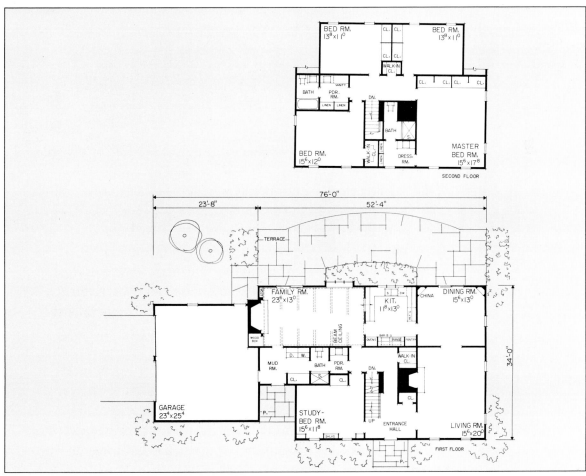

BED RM. 13⁸x11⁰

BED RM. 13⁸x11⁰

CL. CL.

CL. CL.

WALK-IN CL.

CL. CL. CL. CL.

BATH

PDR. RM.

VANITY

LINEN LINEN

DN.

WALK-IN CL.

LINEN LINEN

BATH

S.

BED RM. 15⁶x12⁰

DRESS. RM.

MASTER BED RM. 15⁶x17⁸

76'-0"

23'-8"

52'-4"

34'-0"

TERRACE

FAMILY RM. 23⁶x13⁰

KIT. 11⁸x13⁰

CHINA

DINING RM. 15⁶x13⁰

BEAM CEILING

WOOD BOX

OVEN

BAR B Q

RANGE

PANTRY

D. W.

MUD RM.

BATH

PDR. RM.

WALK-IN CL.

CL.

S.

CL.

DN.

CL.

GARAGE 23⁴x25⁴

P.

STUDY- BED RM. 15⁶x11⁸

SHLVS.

UP

ENTRANCE HALL

LIVING RM. 15⁶x20⁰

FIRST FLOOR

P.

First floor:
1,301 square feet
Second floor:
839 square feet

The utter simplicity of this center-hall Colonial derives from its lean-to profile—the classic saltbox is its ancestor. The trim pedimented entrance, with its six-paneled door, is the only decoration; this house is clean and spare. The massive center chimney opens in two directions—to the formal living room and to the expansive gathering room. This room is particularly appealing to a family that loves to entertain indoors and out. Two sets of sliding glass doors lead from the gathering room to the terrace—a perfect set-up for parties large and small. The kitchen sets aside an intimate corner for cozy family meals. Children can snack here and do homework while parents prepare dinner. There are two bedrooms upstairs, each with its own bath. The stair hall upstairs can be furnished with chairs or a settee to function as a lounge, or set up with a desk for a home office.

The entrance is made gracious by the open, winding staircase.

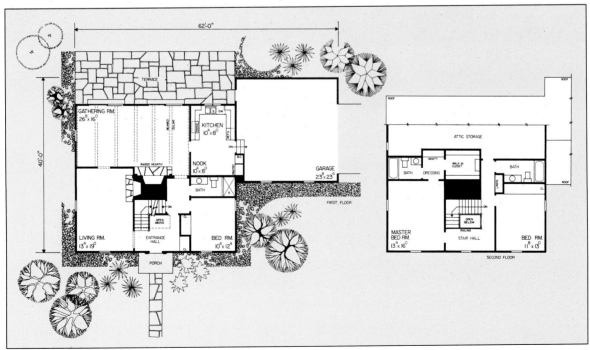

First floor:
1,819 square feet
Greenhouse:
78 square feet
Second floor:
1,472 square feet

Two chimney stacks brace this manor-style center-hall Colonial. Nine-over-six windows and a striking double-leaf front doorway with broken pediment distinguish the gracious facade. The house, however, resonates distinctly to a contemporary lifestyle: A media room, a hobby room, and a greenhouse will attract the family that enjoys myriad activities. The hobby room, for example, is a handyman's delight, with a work island and plenty of space to set up shop. After indulging in all these leisure pursuits, the parents of the house can steep in their overscaled whirlpool—what a luxurious addition to the master bath! The greenhouse is not only a gardener's dream but, in a most practical fashion, harnesses light even on the dimmest days. Ingenious storage solutions enhance the liveability of the house. In the country kitchen a pantry is set in next to the wall ovens. A broom closet is positioned near the doorway to the hobby room, making it completely accessible for clean-up in either room.

A greenhouse, attached to the spacious country kitchen, provides sunlight and ideal conditions for indoor gardening.

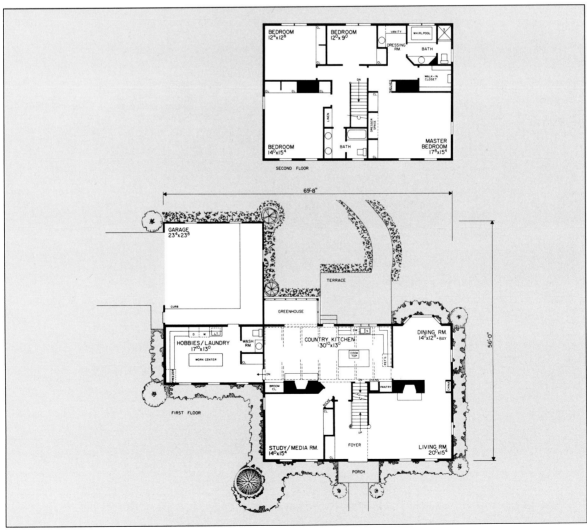

First floor:
1,415 square feet
Second floor:
1,106 square feet

*T*he ingenious sawtooth-shaped side wing or family-room wing of this center-hall Colonial adds flair to an otherwise traditional exterior. Yet the wing is beautifully integrated into the design because its roofline adjoins the rear saltbox sweep. There are two chimneys; the one serving the family room and the study opens to back-to-back fireplaces. The cheerful study also boasts a handsome built-in bookcase wall. The kitchen is centrally located between the dining room and breakfast nook. Both of these rooms open to the back terrace via sliding glass doors. The barnlike rear ell houses the garage, which accesses both the house (through the mudroom) and the backyard. A tiny covered porch off the garage provides protection against rain and snow. Upstairs, the master suite reaches into the side wing to ensure privacy for parents in their bathing and dressing domain. Tucked into the bathing area is a window seat so the adults of the household can daydream, reflect, or read—far from the bustle of family activities.

A study located downstairs contains a corner fireplace and a wall lined with built-in book-shelves.

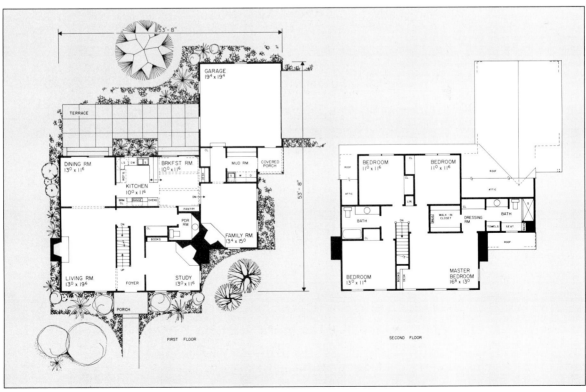

FIRST FLOOR

SECOND FLOOR

First floor:

1,039 square feet

Second floor:

973 square feet

This center-hall Colonial, with its enormous shuttered windows and transom-lit entry, is a traditional and refined classic, yet offers glorious liveability. The entrance hall leads straight back to the generous kitchen which, in turn, pulls light—via a big bank of windows over the sink—back into the hall. The breakfast nook in the kitchen opens to a small patio out back that can also be used for dining al fresco. To the left of the entry is the living room and to the right is the dead-ended, tranquil study. The living room opens directly to the dining room; pocket doors can be installed if the parents of the house want to close off the dining room during an intimate dinner with friends. The garage, which opens both to the house via a mudroom and to the backyard, is an easy pass-through for the gardener. Upstairs in the house, two bedrooms share a bath between them—convenient and private.

The kitchen walls are angled to accommodate a total of five windows overlooking the backyard and terrace.

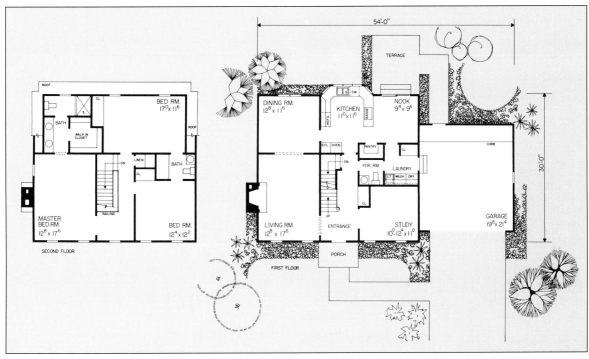

First floor:
1,152 square feet
Second floor:
844 square feet

The single, massive gable extending past the steeply pitched roof on this center-hall saltbox accommodates an extra, separate bedroom that can easily be converted to a lounge, hobby room, or a second study. The refined architectural details on the facade of the house and attached garage signal an affection for our Georgian heritage. Note especially the curved pediment over the box-paneled garage door. To the rear of the garage, contiguous to the backyard, is a garden storage room; it has its own access to the yard and can be closed off during the winter. Inside amenities include a special conversation corner in the snug breakfast room. Shelves are provided throughout the house to supplement closets and closed storage areas. Such shelves can be tailored to accommodate collections and family heirlooms as well.

168

Built-in shelves for storage are located alongside the fireplace in the living room.

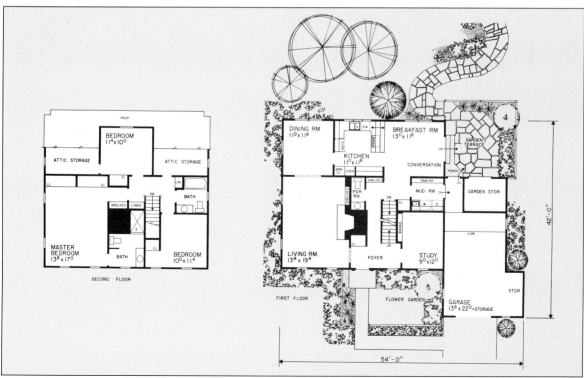

SECOND FLOOR

FIRST FLOOR

First floor:
1,386 square feet
Second floor:
1,232 square feet

The skillfully rendered, pilastered and pedimented front doorway of this center-hall Colonial shows architectural details reminiscent of the Federal era. A graceful fanlight over the door draws light into the entrance hall. The entire rear portion of the house is given over to casual living. The breakfast room and kitchen open directly to the beamed family room. The formal living room, by contrast, is a tranquil enclave. Here, parents can entertain their friends without interruption from children. In the kitchen, a special feature is the walk-in pantry, a mother's dream as it organizes food without inducing clutter. Upstairs, the master suite is lit by five windows, one of which is in the dressing-bath area. The other three bedrooms on the second story share a huge bath. The attic stairs act as a buffer zone between two of the bedrooms.

The classic design of the front door is featured in the gracious entrance to the house.

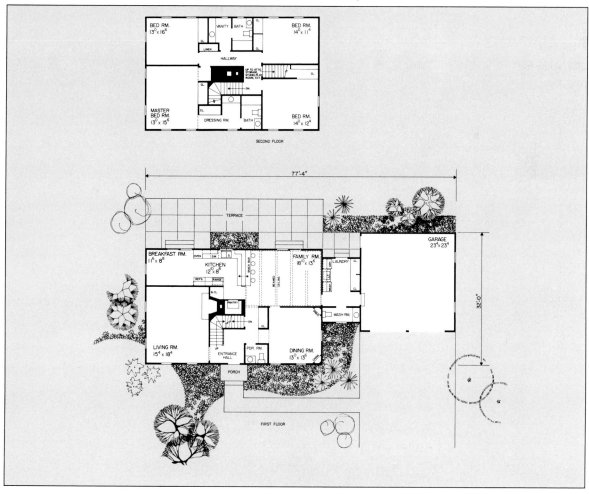

SECOND FLOOR

FIRST FLOOR

First floor:
1,368 square feet
Second floor:
1,046 square feet

This center-hall Colonial, a saltbox, makes up for any potentially lost space in the upper story by adding a house-wide gabled extension that reaches past the pitch of the roof. The extension enwraps both upstairs baths as well as a walk-in closet—and even a third bedroom! All of the multipaned windows have been amplified in scale—enlarged to full 12-over-12s so there is no dearth of light indoors. The living room flows easily and neatly from the entrance hall and extends the full depth of the house. The kitchen and its adjoining breakfast nook step down to the family room. Only a rail separates these two areas, so the entire family always feels comfortable moving about and talking with each other, even if each member of the family is engaged in a different activity. Another family-oriented touch: a long, low hearth that can be banked with pillows for gathering close to the fire in the family room.

Two windows in the dining room overlook the front yard of the house.

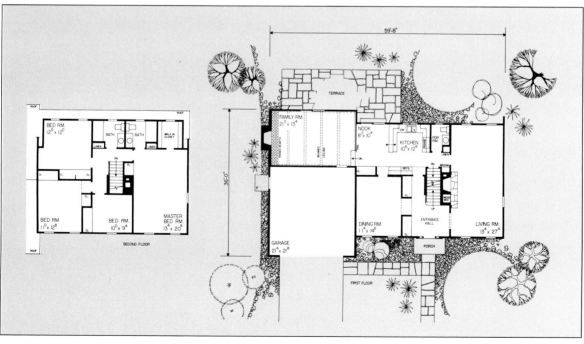

First floor:

1,503 square feet

Second floor:

1,095 square feet

A subtle gable extension at the rear of the second story of this center-hall Colonial extends the private domain of the family past the sloping roof. This ensures plenty of extra living space upstairs, as well as lots of light. Fully one-third of this second floor is given over to the parents of the household, who will relish and enjoy the dressing room, second vanity, and walk-in closet. Two linen closets aid in sorting bedding and towels for each member of the family. The chimney of this Colonial is set slightly off center to free up the commodious center hall, which soars two stories in height. Behind the stairs lies the powder room, centrally located to serve all downstairs rooms with equal convenience. Bonus: All the first-floor windows reach almost to the floor—another architectural solution to pulling in light.

Adjacent to the gracious entry, a powder room is tucked in behind the staircase.

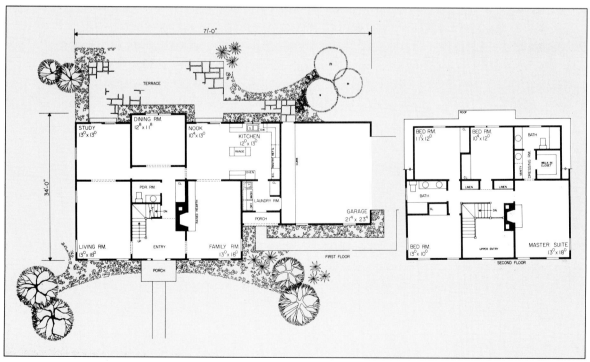

First floor:
1,306 square feet

Second floor:
1,360 square feet

This garrison-style center-hall Colonial combines fieldstone and wide horizontal plank siding to invigorate the design of the facade of this dwelling. Nine-over-nine windows drop almost to the floor to pull in light under the overhang. The single chimney opens to the family room to the right of the entry. As the stairs rise from the entrance hall to the second floor, the rail opens for a more spacious atmosphere upstairs. This feeling can be enhanced by the removal of the wall separating the hall from the study to create a lounge or sitting room in the upstairs hall. (In this eventuality, the door from this lounge to the master bedroom would be sealed off.) Conversely, if the parents want to create a truly private sanctuary out of this room, they could dead-end the room by walling up the door into the hall. Two linen closets upstairs segregate bedding and towels—one for parents, one for children.

The fieldstone used on the exterior can also be applied to the fireplace in the family room.

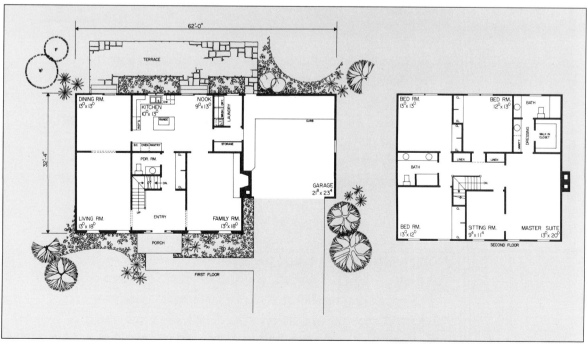

First floor:
1,818 square feet
Greenhouse:
147 square feet
Second floor:
1,395 square feet

Allusions to medieval design motifs, most notably the diamond-pane windows, characterize this garrison-style center-hall Colonial. The roof also sweeps down at the rear of the house in a manner evocative of saltbox design. At the rear of the house, a spacious greenhouse connects the country kitchen with an enormous "clutter" room devoted to hobbies and laundry. The avid green thumb will be enchanted by the greenhouse, where cuttings and seedlings can be nurtured before being transplanted to the garden. There are three fireplaces in this house, two stacked one over the other (for the living room downstairs and the master bedroom up) and the third at the focal point of the country kitchen. The area around this fireplace can be allocated to dining or used as a sitting area, as desired. A window seat in the kitchen looks out into the greenhouse—a perfect spot for daydreaming.

Alongside the fireplace in the large country kitchen lies the entrance to the greenhouse.

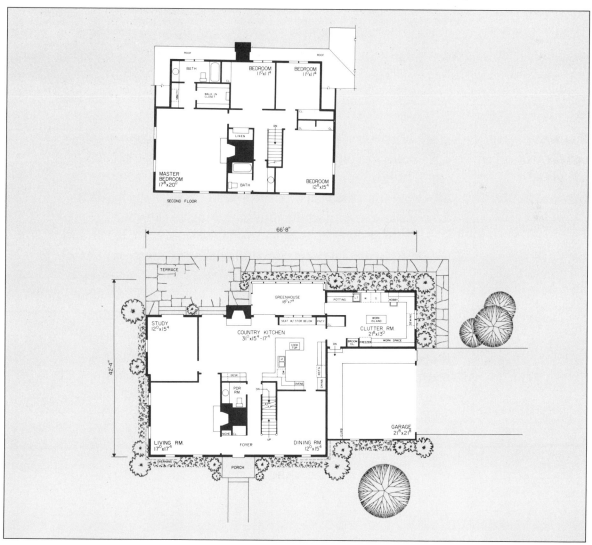

First floor:
1,480 square feet
Second floor:
1,172 square feet

The garrison projection of this center-hall Colonial, plus a long covered porch running alongside the garage and laundry-mudroom, supply protection and shade during months either too hot or too chill. The garage has been turned slightly at an angle, thus garnering an extra storage nook at the back of the garage itself. Inside the front door, the entrance is flanked by two closets, one of which can be reserved just for guests. In the kitchen, the area set aside for eating can easily be outfitted with a desk and coordinating accessories to function as a home office. The dining room, then, would be the central eating location for the family. Upstairs are five bedrooms, so there is enough room for everyone. One or more of these bedrooms can be turned into general play zones or hobby centers. The master bedroom can take over the room adjacent, adding a door between, to create a separate upstairs study.

The long living room, with a traditional fireplace, contains ample room for a comfortable sitting area and a grand piano.

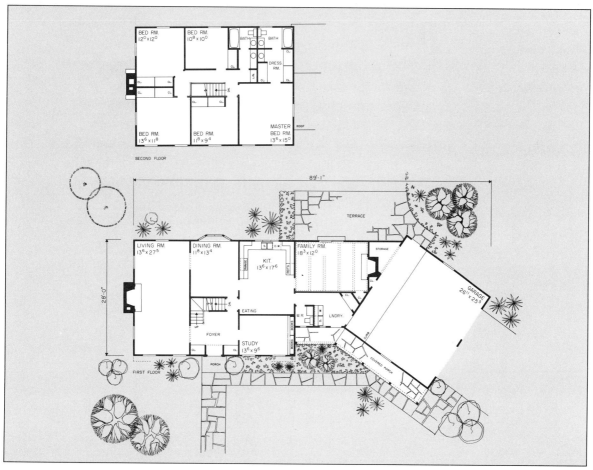

SECOND FLOOR

FIRST FLOOR

First floor:
1,836 square feet

Second floor:
1,232 square feet

The basic structures comprising this center-hall Colonial—house, family room link, and garage wing—would admirably suit a corner lot, as the garage faces away from the side of the house. The family room and laundry are appropriately proportioned to accommodate any number of activities. In the kitchen, a work island is a boon, both as a preparation surface and as a serving center. The entry hall and upstairs hall are dramatized by a curving staircase. Of the four upstairs bedrooms, one has been designated a study, but it can easily be used as a hobby room, playroom, or additional bedroom. A special energy-conscious bonus for this house is its foyer or vestibule, which traps cold air in the winter. The vestibule has a seat and closet so all wet or muddy gear can be left outside the main house.

A curving staircase dramatizes the entry and upstairs halls.

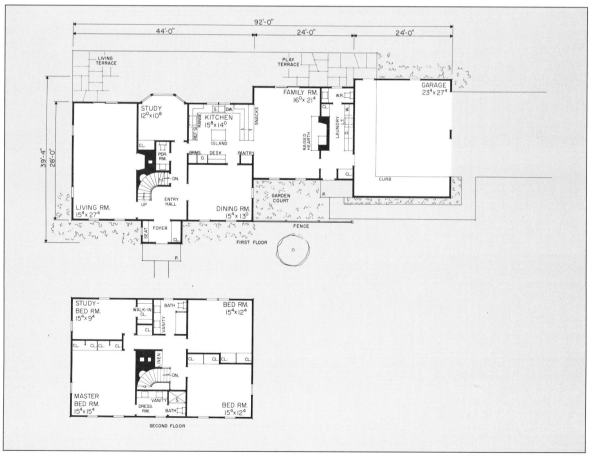

FIRST FLOOR

STUDY
12⁰x10⁸

KITCHEN
15⁸x14⁰

FAMILY RM.
16⁰x21⁴

GARAGE
23⁴x27⁴

LIVING TERRACE

PLAY TERRACE

LIVING RM.
15⁴x27⁴

DINING RM.
15⁴x13⁰

GARDEN COURT

ENTRY HALL

FOYER

SNACKS

LAUNDRY

RAISED HEARTH

CURB

PANTRY

PDR. RM.

DESK

BRMS

ISLAND

REF'G

RANGE

FENCE

SEAT

92'-0"
44'-0"
24'-0"
24'-0"
39'-4"
28'-0"

SECOND FLOOR

STUDY-BED RM.
15⁴x9⁴

BED RM.
15⁴x12⁴

MASTER BED RM.
15⁴x15⁴

BED RM.
15⁴x12⁴

WALK-IN CL.

BATH

VANITY

LINEN

DRESS. RM.

VANITY

BATH

183

First floor:
1,501 square feet
Second floor:
1,280 square feet

Under the roof cornice of this clapboarded center-hall Colonial you'll find a series of "eyebrow" windows—abbreviated windows that recall Colonial antecedents. These windows are set at the standard height, not near the floor, so that tables and other pieces of furniture can be set in front of them. The two fireplaces in this house neatly stack one over the other; the lower fireplace is the focal point in the formal living room and the upper one warms the master bedroom. The master bedroom extends into a lounge that can be shared with all members of the family or can be closed off as a truly private retreat. After a long day, working parents will relish a sanctuary of their very own.

The master bedroom upstairs contains a fireplace and connects to a lounge.

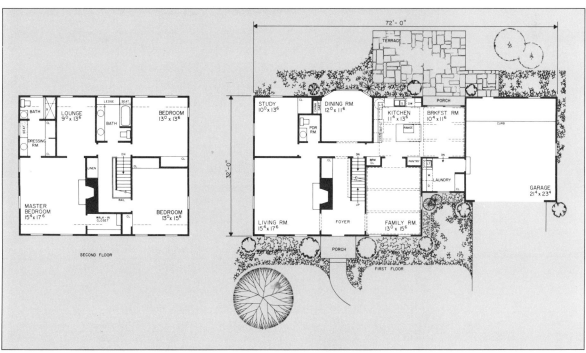

SECOND FLOOR

FIRST FLOOR

First floor:
1,408 square feet
Second floor:
1,408 square feet

The gambrel roof of this center-hall Colonial lifts the house to accommodate an optional third floor—and the roofline is echoed by that over the garage. The approach to the house is highlighted by a pedimented portico and by a fence protecting the flowerbeds on either side of the entry. The grand entrance hall, punctuated by a graceful staircase, opens conveniently to the living room on the left and beamed family room on the right. Both living room and family room boast fireplaces; the one in the family room has a handy woodbox alongside the fireplace cavity. The living and dining rooms are separated by narrow cabinets that are prescribed for books, but could hold more pieces of treasured china to complement the display in the corner cupboards in the dining room. The stair hall upstairs can be fitted out with a window seat, thus transforming the space into a lounge for the entire family. Four large bedrooms and two baths complete the plan.

The living room, with its corner fireplace, is adjacent to the dining room. Built-in cabinets flank the passage that connects the two rooms.

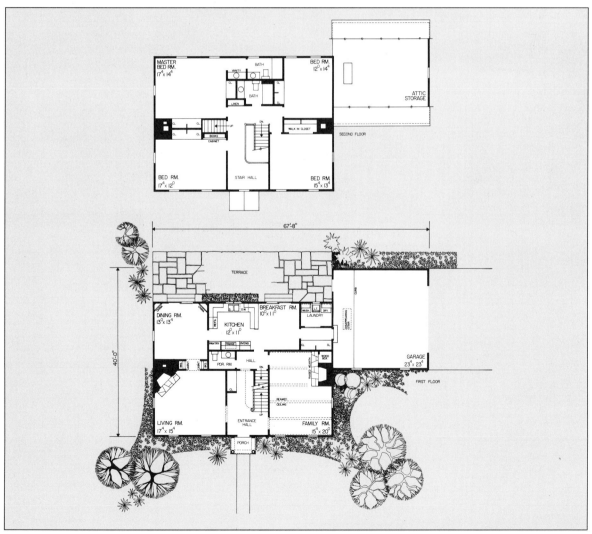

First floor:
1,023 square feet
Second floor:
1,008 square feet
Third floor:
476 square feet

This center-hall Colonial, with its pedimented entry, presents a patrician facade while, at the rear, it opens up to informality and joyous indoor-outdoor liveability. The house offers three stories of living space. The attic story is devoted to quiet pursuits away from the hubbub of the rest of the house. On the ground floor, spaces are evenly divided—formal and informal. The kitchen is particularly efficient, as its work area branches onto a wide peninsula that functions as a serving counter for the adjoining breakfast area. The parents of the household will be drawn to the desk area, where they can monitor children's activities as well as keep up with their own personal endeavors. In the master bedroom, a bank of shelves supplements the closets.

In the dining room a gracious bay window overlooks the backyard.

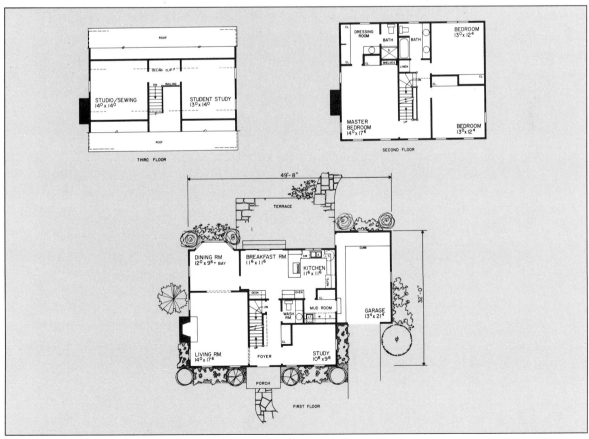

STUDIO/SEWING
14⁰ x 14⁰

STUDENT STUDY
13⁰ x 14⁰

THIRD FLOOR

DRESSING ROOM

BEDROOM
13⁰ x 12⁴

MASTER BEDROOM
14⁰ x 17⁶

BEDROOM
13⁰ x 12⁴

SECOND FLOOR

49'-8"

TERRACE

DINING RM.
12⁰ x 9⁶ + BAY

BREAKFAST RM.
11⁶ x 11⁶

KITCHEN
11⁶ x 11⁶

OVEN

MUD ROOM

WASH RM

GARAGE
13⁴ x 21⁴

32'-0"

LIVING RM.
14⁰ x 17⁶

FOYER

STUDY
10⁸ x 9⁸

PORCH

FIRST FLOOR

First floor:
1,440 square feet

Second floor:
1,280 square feet

The traditional lines of this clapboarded center-hall Colonial are set off by equally traditional—and time-honored—architectural details: a massive chimney, a recessed entry with transom, and full-length shutters bracketing the 12-over-12 windows. The casual family room and kitchen at the back of the house look out to the terrace and backyard. A secondary chimney abuts the family room; the fireplace in this room is flanked by built-in bookcases, one of which caps a recessed woodbox. A family that enjoys entertaining on a formal scale will applaud the study across the entry from the living room. This room is a tranquil place to serve tea or after-dinner coffee and cordials—the cabinet under the bookshelf is a perfect serving center. In the master suite upstairs, the bath is set into a tiled alcove, a lovely hideaway for relaxing—perhaps in a bubblebath!

Built-in bookcases and counter line one wall of the study downstairs, a room that can also be used as an extra bedroom.

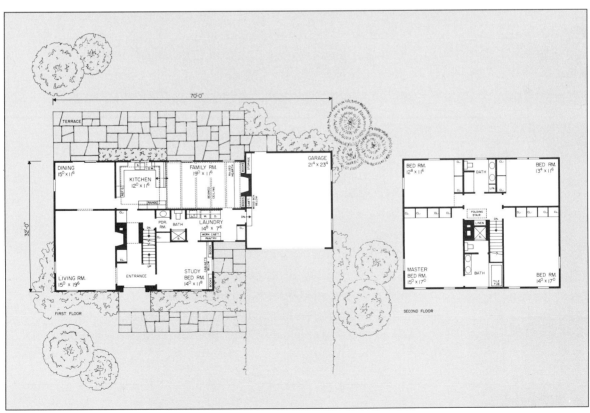

First floor:
1,505 square feet
Second floor:
1,344 square feet

Buttressed by a pair of massive chimneys, this traditional center-hall Colonial presents an imposing, but never intimidating, facade. The door and windows are boldly outlined by exquisitely detailed trim; the front door is further dramatized by a transom-light surround. The entrance hall is tiled throughout. A large closet is a welcome amenity in this space. The house is anchored by a huge eat-in kitchen. The eating area, embraced by a room-wide window bay, cannot help but be flooded with light. Next to this area and convenient to the kitchen is the family room, which centers on a fireplace. An active family will appreciate the extra storage room off the garage, handy for storing bicycles and outdoor gear—or ideal as a workshop for a handy adult. The garage accesses to the house via a mudroom that also houses laundry equipment. There are four bedrooms upstairs. The master bedroom can be opened to the room adjacent to create a private in-house office or lounge.

A tiled floor dramatizes the gracious entrance to the house.

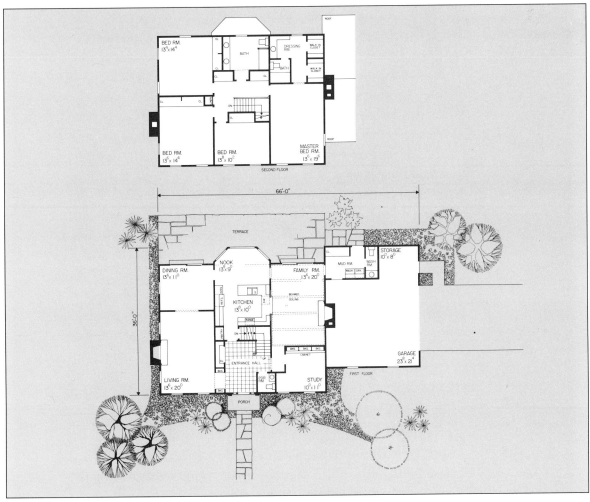

PLAN B2963

First floor:
2,028 square feet
Second floor:
1,516 square feet

Featuring a gracious foyer and stairway at the entry, this home in the Colonial tradition is actually a modified version of the center-hall classic. Unlike the classic standard, the entrance here is off-center in the facade, with three windows to the left and two to the right of the entry door. Yet the design offers the dignity and grace so readily associated with its center-hall cousin. In addition, the rambling proportions of the house reflect Colonial precedents—as families grew, so did their houses. The side and back of the house feature an unusual combination of windows: a large bow window in the living room faces the fireplace; tall bay windows in the downstairs study are repeated in the upstairs master bedroom; and a modified bay window in the kitchen wraps around the counter. Both the dining and living rooms boast large fireplaces, features that enhance the charm and liveability of these two rooms. Family meals are likely to be served in the cozy nook attached to the kitchen, where bright sunlight is softened by the porch roof at the back of the house. Ample cabinet, shelf, and pantry space is provided wherever storage space is most needed. To retreat from the clamor of an active household, family members can read a good book in the study tucked in behind the living room, where generous provision is made for an entire library. Upstairs, four bedrooms provide a comfortable arrangement for each family member. Here, there's also an option for extending the spacious master bedroom into a master suite.

The spacious living room is located off the entry, very much in the tradition of the parlor, where visitors were entertained by their hosts.

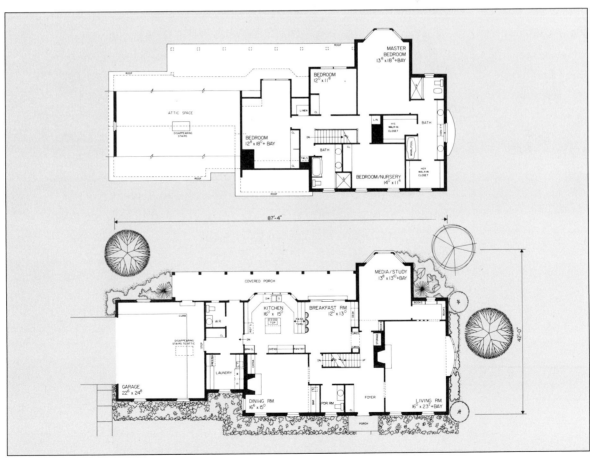

First floor:
1,543 square feet
Second floor:
1,005 square feet

Turning this center-hall Colonial on the L guarantees a sense of privacy in a closely knit neighborhood. This house adapts well to a corner lot, as the front entry faces one street and the garage the cross-street. The court formed by the L is demarcated by a picket fence, as is the garage turnaround. The tiled foyer branches into the living room and family room, and to the study beyond the living room. Both the family room and the kitchen sport beamed ceilings. The kitchen is a single-story link to the garage and a sure focus for an active family. Note the eating area set near the big window facing the court. Four bedrooms upstairs, with two baths, complete this interesting plan.

Two large windows or sliding doors in the dining room overlook the grand terrace and backyard.

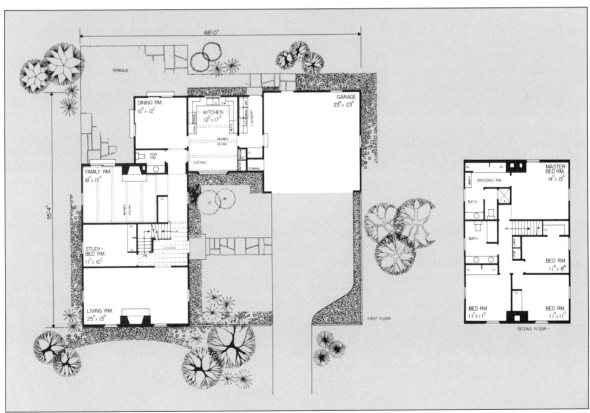

Selecting the most suitable house plan for your family is a matter of matching your needs, tastes, and lifestyle with one of the many designs offered here. When you study the floor plans and blueprints you may subsequently order, remember that they are simply two-dimensional representations of what will eventually be a three-dimensional reality.

Floor plans are easy to read. Rooms are clearly labeled, with dimensions given in feet and inches. Most symbols are logical and self-explanatory: the location of bathroom fixtures, planters, fireplaces, tile floors, cabinets and counters, sinks, appliances, closets, sloped or beamed ceilings will be obvious.

A blueprint, although much more detailed, is also easy to read; all it demands is concentration. The blueprints offered here come in many large sheets, each one of which contains a different kind of information. One sheet contains foundation and excavation drawings; another has a precise plot plan. An elevations sheet deals with the exterior walls of the house; section drawings show precise dimensions, fittings, doors, windows, and roof structures. Detailed floor plans give the construction information needed by your contractor. Separate from the blueprints, but an important part of the package is a lengthy materials list, with sizes and quantities of all necessary components. Using this list, a contractor and suppliers can help calculate costs for you.

When you first study a floor plan or blueprint, imagine that you are walking through the house. By visualizing each room in three dimensions, you can transform the technical data and symbols into something more real.

Start at the front door. It's preferable to have a foyer or entrance hall in which to receive guests. A closet here is desirable; a powder room is a plus.

Look for good traffic circulation. You should not have to pass all the way through one main room to reach another. From the entrance area you should have direct access to the three principal areas of a house—the living, working, and sleeping zones. For example, a foyer might provide separate entrances to the living room, kitchen, patio, and a hallway or staircase leading to the bedrooms.

Study the layout of each zone. Most people expect the living room to be protected from cross traffic. The kitchen, on the other hand, should connect with the dining room—with perhaps the utility room, basement, garage, patio or deck, or a secondary entrance. A homemaker whose workday centers in the kitchen may have special requirements: a window that faces the backyard; a clear view of the family room where children play; a garage or driveway entrance that allows for a short trip with groceries; or laundry facilities close at hand. Check for efficient placement of kitchen cabinets, counters, and appliances. Is there enough room in the kitchen for eating? Is there a dining nook?

Perhaps this part of the house contains a family room or a den-bedroom-office. It's advantageous to have a bathroom or powder room in this section.

As you study the plan, you may enounter a staircase, indicated by a group of parallel lines—the number of lines equaling the number of steps. An arrow labeled "up" means that the staircase leads to a higher level, and one pointing down means it leads to a lower level. Staircases in a split-level will have both up and down arrows on one staircase because the two main levels are depicted in one drawing and any extra levels in another.

Notice the location of the stairways. Is too much floor space lost to them? Will you find yourself making too many trips?

Study the sleeping quarters. Are the bedrooms situated as you like? You may want the master bedroom near the children, or you may want it as far away as possible. Is there at least one closet per person in each bedroom or a double one for a couple? Bathrooms should be convenient to each bedroom—if not adjoining, then with hallway access and on the same floor.

Once you are familiar with the relative positions of the rooms, look for such structural details as:

• sufficient uninterrupted wall space for furniture arrangement;
• adequate room dimensions;
• potential heating or cooling problems—that is, a room over a garage or next to the laundry;
• window and door placement for good ventilation and natural light;
• location of doorways—avoid having a basement staircase or a bathroom in view of the dining room;
• adequate auxiliary space—closets, storage, bathrooms, countertops;
• separation of activity areas. Will noise from the recreation room disturb sleeping children or a parent at work?

As you complete your mental walk through the house, bear in mind your family's long-range needs. A good house plan will allow for some adjustments now and additions in the future.

Each member of your family may find the listing of his or her favorite features a most helpful exercise. Why not try it?

A contractor is part craftsman, part businessman, and part magician. As the person who will transform your dreams and drawings into a finished house, he will be responsible for the budget for the structure, for the quality of the workmanship, and for the solving of all problems that occur quite naturally in the course of construction. Choose him as carefully as you would a business partner.

There are two types of residential contractors: the *construction company* and the *carpenter-builder*, often called a general contractor. Each of these has its advantages and disadvantages.

The carpenter-builder works directly on the job as the field foreman. Because his background is that of a craftsman, his workmanship is probably good—but his paperwork may be slow or sloppy. His overhead—which you pay for—is less than that of a large construction company. However, if the job drags on beyond schedule for any reason, his interest may flag because your project is overlapping his next job and eroding his profits.

Construction companies handle several projects simultaneously. They have an office staff to keep the paperwork moving and an army of subcontractors they know they can count on. Though you are normally assured that they will meet deadlines, they may sacrifice workmanship in order to do so. Because they emphasize efficiency, they are less personal to work with than a general contractor. Many will not work with an individual unless he is represented by an architect.

To find a reliable contractor, start by asking friends who have built homes or additions to their homes. Check with local lumberyards and building-supply outlets for names of possible candidates.

Once you have several names in hand, ask the Chamber of Commerce, Better Business Bureau, or local department of consumer affairs for any information they might have on each of them.

Set up an interview with each of the potential candidates. Ask to see projects that are completed as well as work in progress, emphasizing that you are interested in projects comparable to yours.

Ask each contractor for bank references from both his commercial bank and any other lender he has worked with. If he is in good financial standing, he should have no qualms about giving you this information. Also ask if he offers a warranty on his work. Most will give you a one-year warranty on the structure; some offer as much as a ten-year warranty.

Ask for references, even though no contractor will give you the name of a dissatisfied customer. While previous clients may be pleased with a contractor's work overall, they may, for example, have had to wait three months after they moved in before they had any closet doors.

Talk to each of the candidates about fees. Most work on a "cost-plus" basis; that is, the basic cost of the project—materials, subcontractors' services, wages of those working directly on the project, but not office help—plus his fee. Some have a fixed fee; others work on a percentage of the basic cost. A fixed fee is usually better for you if you can get one. If a contractor works on a percentage, ask for a cost breakdown of the best estimate and keep very careful track as the work progresses. A crafty contractor can always use a cost overrun to his advantage when working on a percentage.

If the top two or three candidates are willing to submit competitive bids, give each a copy of the plans and your specifications for materials. If they are not each working from the same guidelines, the competitive bids will be of little value. Give each the same deadline for turning in a bid; two or three weeks is a reasonable period of time.

Though the above method sounds very fair and orderly, it is not always the best approach, especially if you are inexperienced. You may want to review the bids with your architect if you have one, or with your lender, to discuss which to accept. They may not recommend the lowest. A low bid does not necessarily mean that you will get quality with economy.

If the bids are relatively close, the most important consideration may not be money at all. How easily you can talk with a contractor and whether or not he inspires confidence are very important considerations for you to take into account.

Once you have financing, you can sign a contract with the builder. Most have their own contract forms, but it is advisable to have a lawyer draw one up and use that rather than the builder's or, at the very least, review the builder's standard contract.

A good contract should include the following:

• plans and sketches of the work to be done, subject to your approval;
• a list of materials, including quantity, brand names, style or serial numbers (do not permit any "or equal" clauses that will allow the contractor to make substitutions);
• the terms—who (you or the lender) pays whom and when;
• a production schedule;
• the contractor's certification of insurance for workmen's compensation, damage, and liability;
• a rider stating that all changes, whether or not they increase the cost, must be submitted and approved in writing.

Of course, this list represents the least a contractor should include. Once you have signed it, your plans are on the way to becoming a home.

Frontal Sheet

Detailed Floor Plans

Foundation Plans

House Cross-Sections

Interior Elevations

Exterior Elevations

Material List

COMPLETE HOME PLANS FOR YOU

The Home Planners Blueprint Package will help you and your family intelligently plan your new home. The time you spend with the detailed plans of your home will be informative and enjoyable. Most important, the plans will help you make the most of the time you spend working with your builder and architect. The Blueprint Package will save you time and money. With each Blueprint Package you will receive detailed architect's blueprints, and a specification outline. A separate materials list is also available.

BLUEPRINTS

FRONTAL SHEET Artist's landscaped sketch of the exterior and ink-line floor plans.

FOUNDATION PLAN Basement and foundation plan in ¼-inch scale, plus plot plan for locating house on building site.

DETAILED FLOOR PLAN First- and second-floor plans in ¼-inch scale, plus cross-section detail keys and layouts of electrical outlets and switches.

HOUSE CROSS-SECTIONS Large-scale sections of foundation, interior and exterior walls, floors, and roof details.

INTERIOR ELEVATIONS Large-scale interior details of kitchen cabinet design, bathrooms, laundry, fireplaces, and built-ins.
EXTERIOR ELEVATIONS Drawings in ¼-inch scale of front, rear, and sides of house.

MATERIALS LIST

For a small additional fee, you'll also receive a materials list. It outlines the quantity, type, and size of the non-mechanical materials required to build your home. It also simplifies your material ordering and gets you quicker and more accurate prices from your builder and hardware dealer.

Includes:

- Masonry, Veneer & Fireplace
- Framing Lumber
- Roofing & Sheet Metal
- Windows & Door Frames
- Exterior Trim & Insulation
- Tile & Flooring
- Interior Trim & Kitchen Cabinets
- Rough & Finish Hardware

Because of differences in geographical regions, local codes, and installation methods, mechanical materials and specifications are not included. Consult local heating, plumbing, and electrical contractors for the necessary materials for your home.

Materials list is $25.00 for any size order. Not sold separately from blueprints.

SPECIFICATION OUTLINE

A 16-page fill-in specification list of more than 150 phases of home construction from excavating to painting will let you tell your builder the exact materials, equipment, and methods of construction you want in your new home.

Includes:

- General Instructions, Suggestions, & Information
- Excavating & Grading
- Masonry
- Concrete Work
- Sheet Metal Work
- Carpentry, Millwork, & Roofing
- Lath & Plaster or Drywall Wallboard
- Schedule for Room Finishes
- Painting & Finishing
- Tile
- Electrical
- Plumbing
- Heating & Air-Conditioning

Additional outlines are $3.00 a copy.

1. STUDY THE DESIGNS

As you review the custom homes in this and other Home Planners books, keep in mind the total living requirements of your family, both indoors and out. Although we do not modify plans for our customers, minor changes can be made before you start construction. If you plan to make major changes, you should order one set of blueprints and have them redrawn locally. Consult with your builder or architect if you plan major changes.

2. HOW TO ORDER BLUEPRINTS

Complete the order form at right and return with your remittance. Credit card and C.O.D. orders are accepted. For C.O.D. shipments, the post office will collect all charges, including postage and C.O.D. fees. C.O.D. shipments are not permitted outside the United States. Telephone orders can be processed and shipped in the next day's mail. Call toll free 1-800-521-6797. Michigan residents call collect 0-313-477-1854.

3. REVERSE BLUEPRINTS

As a special service to those wishing to build in reverse of the plan as shown, Home Planners offers reverse blueprints at a cost of $25.00 additional per set with each order. Although the lettering and dimensions appear backwards, reverse blueprints are a valuable reference because they show the house as it's actually being built.

4. EXCHANGE POLICY

Since blueprints are printed in response to individual orders, blueprint materials are not returnable. However, the first set of blueprints in any order, or the one set in a single-set order, may be exchanged for a set of another design for $20.00 plus $3.00 postage and handling via surface mail; $4.00 for priority mail.

HOW MANY SETS OF BLUEPRINTS WILL YOU NEED?

A single set of blueprints of your favorite design is sufficient if you plan to study the house in greater detail. However, if you are planning to get estimates or to build, you may need as many as eight sets of blueprints. You can save by planning your order carefully and ordering your total requirements now. The first set of blueprints is $125.00, and additional sets of the same design in each order are $30.00. To determine the number of sets you will need, use the check list below.

____ OWNER'S SET
____ BUILDER (usually requires 3 sets: legal, inspection, tradesperson)
____ BUILDING PERMIT (occasionally requires 2 sets)
____ MORTGAGE SOURCE (usually 1 set for conventional; 3 sets for F.H.A. and V.A.)
____ REVIEW BOARD OR SUBDIVISION COMMITTEE
____ TOTAL NUMBER OF SETS REQUIRED

BLUEPRINT ORDERING HOTLINE PHONE TOLL FREE 1-800-521-6797

Orders received by 11 a.m. (Eastern time) will be processed the same day and shipped the following day. Michigan residents call collect 0-313-477-1854.

NOTE: When ordering by phone, please mention the Order Form Key Number located in the box at the lower left corner of the blueprint order form.

In Canada, add 20% to all prices on the accompanying order form, and remit in Canadian funds to:
HOME PLANNERS, INC.
20 Cedar Street North
Kitchener, Ontario N2H 2W8
Phone: 519-743-4169

HOME PLANNERS, INC., 23761 Research Drive, Farmington Hills, MI 48024

Please rush me the following:

____ SET(S) BLUEPRINTS FOR DESIGN NO(S). _____ $_____
    Single Set, $125.00; Additional Identical Sets in Same Order $30.00 ea.
    4 Set Package of Same Design, $175.00 (Save $40.00)
    8 Set Package of Same Design, $225.00 (Save $110.00)

| Canadian customers add |
| 20% to all prices. Mail in |
| Canadian funds to the ad- |
| dress on the opposite page. |

____ MATERIALS LIST just $25.00 for Entire Order
    (1 List per Set and 1 Specification Outline included) $_____
____ SPECIFICATION OUTLINES @ $3.00 EACH $_____

Michigan Residents add 4% sales tax $_____

FOR POSTAGE
AND HANDLING
PLEASE CHECK
✔ & REMIT

☐ $3.00 Added to Order for Surface Mail (UPS)—Any Order
☐ $4.00 Added for Priority Mail of One to Three Sets of Blueprints
☐ $6.00 Added for Priority Mail of Four or more Sets of Blueprints $_____
☐ For Canadian orders add $2.00 to above applicable rates

☐ C.O.D. PAY POSTMAN (C.O.D. Within U.S.A. Only)   TOTAL in U.S.A. funds $_____

PLEASE PRINT
Name _____
Street _____
City _____ State _____ Zip _____

CREDIT CARD ORDERS ONLY: Fill in the Boxes below.   Prices subject to change without notice.

Credit
Card No. ☐☐☐☐☐☐☐☐☐☐☐☐☐☐☐☐

Expiration Date
Month/Year ☐☐☐☐

CHECK ONE: ☐ **VISA** ☐ **MasterCard**

Order Form Key
TBIIBP

Your Signature _____

BLUEPRINT ORDERS SHIPPED WITHIN 48 HOURS OF RECEIPT!

HOME PLANNERS, INC., 23761 Research Drive, Farmington Hills, MI 48024

Please rush me the following:

____ SET(S) BLUEPRINTS FOR DESIGN NO(S). _____ $_____
    Single Set, $125.00; Additional Identical Sets in Same Order $30.00 ea.
    4 Set Package of Same Design, $175.00 (Save $40.00)
    8 Set Package of Same Design, $225.00 (Save $110.00)

| Canadian customers add |
| 20% to all prices. Mail in |
| Canadian funds to the ad- |
| dress on the opposite page. |

____ MATERIALS LIST just $25.00 for Entire Order
    (1 List per Set and 1 Specification Outline included) $_____
____ SPECIFICATION OUTLINES @ $3.00 EACH $_____

Michigan Residents add 4% sales tax $_____

FOR POSTAGE
AND HANDLING
PLEASE CHECK
✔ & REMIT

☐ $3.00 Added to Order for Surface Mail (UPS)—Any Order
☐ $4.00 Added for Priority Mail of One to Three Sets of Blueprints
☐ $6.00 Added for Priority Mail of Four or more Sets of Blueprints $_____
☐ For Canadian orders add $2.00 to above applicable rates

☐ C.O.D. PAY POSTMAN (C.O.D. Within U.S.A. Only)   TOTAL in U.S.A. funds $_____

PLEASE PRINT
Name _____
Street _____
City _____ State _____ Zip _____

CREDIT CARD ORDERS ONLY: Fill in the Boxes below.   Prices subject to change without notice.

Credit
Card No. ☐☐☐☐☐☐☐☐☐☐☐☐☐☐☐☐

Expiration Date
Month/Year ☐☐☐☐

CHECK ONE: ☐ **VISA** ☐ **MasterCard**

Order Form Key
TBIIBP

Your Signature _____

ADDITIONAL PLAN BOOKS

THE DESIGN CATEGORY SERIES

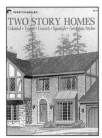

360 Two Story Homes
English Tudors, Early American Salt Boxes, Gambrels, Farmhouses, Southern Colonials, Georgians, French Mansards, Contemporaries. Floor plans for small and large families. Two to 6 bedrooms, family rooms, libraries, extra baths, mudrooms. Homes for all budgets. 288 Pages, $6.95

(1)

150 1½ Story Homes
Cape Cod, Williamsburg, Georgian, Tudor, Contemporaries. Low-budget and country-estate feature sections. Expandable family plans. Formal and informal living and dining areas. Spacious country kitchens. Indoor-outdoor liveability with covered porches and functional terraces. 128 Pages, $3.95

(2)

210 One Story Homes Over 2,000 Sq. Ft.
Spanish, Western, Tudor, French, Contemporaries. Family rooms, separate dining rooms, atriums, efficient kitchens, laundries. Designs from modest to country-estate budgets. 192 Pages, $4.95

(3)

315 One Story Homes Under 2,000 Sq. Ft.
An outstanding selection of traditional and contemporary exteriors for medium and restricted budgets. Efficient, practical floor plans. Gathering rooms, formal and informal living and dining rooms, mudrooms, indoor-outdoor liveability. Economy homes. 192 Pages, $4.95

(4)

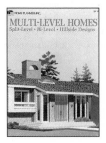

215 Multi-Level Homes
A large variety of exterior styles and floor plans for flat and sloping sites. Exposed lower levels. Balconies and decks. Upper-level lounges. Sloping ceilings. Functional outdoor terraces. 192 Pages, $4.95

(5)

223 Vacation Homes
A-Frames, Chalets, Hexagons, and designs with decks, balconies, and terraces. Oriented for flat and sloping sites. Spacious, open planning for lakeshore or woodland living. Sleeping for 2 to 22. Lodges for summer and winter use. 176 Pages, $4.95

(6)

OTHER CURRENT TITLES

330 Early American Home Plans
Complete collection of Early American and Traditional homes in one magnificent book! Traces Early American architecture from colonial times to traditional styles popular today. An outstanding array of Gambrels, Salt Boxes, Cape Cods, Georgian and Federal variations, Southern Colonials, Farmhouses and Country Estate houses. 304 Pages, $9.95

(7)

335 Contemporary Home Plans
The definitive statement on modern and functional home designs. Offers a colorful guide to modern architecture, including a history of contemporary American styling. Features Solar-Oriented Trend Houses, Earth-Sheltered Homes and Atrium Designs, as well as imaginative plans for one-, 1½-, two-story and multi-level Contemporaries. 304 Pages, $9.95

(8)

(9)

Encyclopedia of Home Designs — 450 Plans

The best-selling home plan encyclopedia of all time! Varying exterior styles plus practical floor plans for all building budgets. Formal-informal traffic patterns. Indoor-outdoor liveability. Small, growing, and large family home plans. One of the largest selections of home plans available in a single volume. Over 1,150 illustrations and lavish use of color.
320 Pages, $9.95

(10)

Most Popular Home Designs

In this case, you *can* tell a book by its cover. This one has 360 time-tested winners. Included are picture-perfect designs that families across the nation have loved to call home. One stories, 1½ stories, two stories, multi-levels. Early American, Colonial, Georgian, Federal, Tudor, French, Spanish, Contemporary. Livable, affordable, expandable. Luxurious, spacious, unbeatably up-scale. They're all here, along with many of today's most-asked-for amenities.
273 pages, $8.95

(11)

Home Plans for Outdoor Living

This superbly produced, 192-page volume showcases more than 100 home designs, each uniquely styled to bring the outdoors in. Terraces. Decks. Porches. Balconies, Court-yards. Atriums. Greenhouses, Garden Rooms, Solariums. Swimming Pools and Spas. All have a place in the book, with practical home plans designed to bring the ideas down to earth and put them to work. Loaded with full-color photos, it contains one-, 1½-, and two-story designs, as well as multi-level plans, in all sizes and styles, including Early American, English Tudor, French, Spanish and Western, and Contemporary. An exciting book for the outdoor lover in everybody.
192 pages, $10.95

(12)

Color Portfolio of Houses & Plans — 310 Designs

An expanded, full-color guide to our most popular Early American, Spanish, French, Tudor, Contemporary, and modern Trend home designs. This eye-popping book contains a total of 310 home plans of all popular styles and sizes. Includes one-, 1½-, and two-story plans, plus multi-level designs suited to all terrains. Features an array of energy-efficient plans, as well as designs for varying building budgets. This is our largest full-color book and includes both our newest designs and best old favorites. It's must reading for the serious home planner.
289 full-color pages, $12.95

HOME PLANNERS, INC. Dept. BK, 23761 Research Drive, Farmington Hills, MI 48024

Please mail me the following:

THE DESIGN CATEGORY SERIES

1. _____ 360 Two Story Homes @ $6.95 ea. $_____
2. _____ 150 1½ Story Homes @ $3.95 ea. $_____
3. _____ 210 One Story Homes over 2,000 Sq. Ft. @ $4.95 $_____
4. _____ 315 One Story Homes Under 2,000 Sq. Ft. @ 4.95 $_____
5. _____ 215 Multi-Level Homes @ $4.95 ea. $_____
6. _____ 223 Vacation Homes @ $4.95 $_____

All 6 Books; over 1,250 designs; 1168 Pages only $19.95 (a $30.70 value; Save $10.75) $_____

OTHER CURRENT TITLES

7. _____ 330 Early American Home Plans @ $9.95 $_____
8. _____ 335 Contemporary Home Plans @ $9.95 $_____
9. _____ 450 House Plans Encyclopedia @ $9.95 ea. $_____
10. _____ 360 Most Popular Home Designs @ $8.95 $_____
11. _____ Home Plans for Outdoor Living @ $10.95 $_____
12. _____ Color Portfolio @ $12.95 $_____

Subtotal $_____
Michigan residents add 4% Sales Tax $_____
Postage and Handling $___1.50___
TOTAL—Check Enclosed $_____

MAIL TODAY—Satisfaction Guaranteed!
Your Order Will Be Processed and Shipped Within 48 Hours!

PLEASE PRINT

Name _____

Address _____

City _____ State _____ Zip _____

In Canada, add 20% to all prices above and mail to:
Home Planners, Inc., 20 Cedar St. North, Kitchener, Ontario N2H 2W8

TB11BK

Balloon framing Type of house framing in which studs in the outer walls run continuously from the sill of the foundation to the roof.

Batten Narrow strip of wood used to cover a joint in vertical siding.

Bay window A framed stucture housing a window, ceiling, and floor in a semi-octagonal plan.

Board-and-batten Vertical siding in the form of boards joined side-by-side with vertical battens covering the joints.

Borning room A room in the house originally reserved for childbirth and illness.

Bow window A framed structure housing a window, ceiling, and floor in a semi-circular plan.

Clapboard Boards used as siding. Applied horizontally, the boards have a 1-inch overlap and are 1/2 inch thick and 12 inches wide.

Clerestory window Fixed narrow, horizontal, or triangular windows, usually placed high on the wall.

Cornice The overhang of a roof.

Cross-buck door Door reinforced by strips of wood attached from corner to corner in a cross.

Cupola A light structure on the roof, originally serving as a belfry, lantern, or viewing post, now a decorative feature.

Dormer window Upright window installed to protrude beyond the slant of the roof.

Double-hung window A sliding window in which two sashes slide up and down vertically in separate tracks.

Dovecote A structure at or near the roof originally designed to house domestic pigeons, now a decorative feature.

Gable roof Pitched roof with equal angles from the ridge beam.

Gambrel roof Roof with two planes on each side of the central ridge beam.

Garrison house A house in which the upper story is overhanging the lower story.

Half house A Cape Cod house, too small to accommodate a family, often called a "honeymoon" house.

Hip roof A roof with planes slanting in four directions from the central ridge beam.

Keeping room Originally the room occupied by a person or family as a sitting room, or parlor, now synonymous with family room.

Panel door Door with raised panels.

Plank door Door constructed from a flush plank or planks of wood.

Pilaster A shallow, rectangular shape projecting from a wall, imitating the form of a column.

Pediment Arched, triangular, or curved decorative shape above the door, common in Colonial architecture.

Platform framing Type of house construction in which subfloors, extending outside the edges of the building, provide platforms onto which the studs are erected.

Pitch Rate of rise or slope to a roof.

Raised panel A panel beveled on all four sides, usually seen in doors.

Ridge beam Central beam at the top of a pitched roof to which all rafters are fastened.

Saltbox house A type of house commonly found in New England, usually two stories in front, with a gable roof continuing downward to cover a low rear section.

INDEX

INDEX TO PLANS